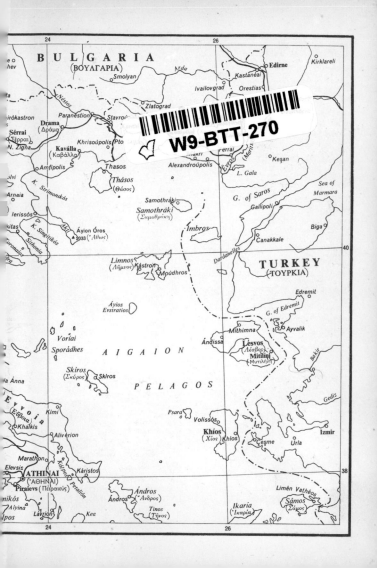

COLLINS
PHRASE BOOKS

GREEK

COLLINS
PHRASE BOOKS

GREEK

Compiled by
CHRISTOPHER SCOTT

COLLINS
LONDON AND GLASGOW

GENERAL EDITOR: J. B. FOREMAN, M.A.
First published 1964
Latest Reprint 1970

PRINTED IN GREAT BRITAIN BY
COLLINS CLEAR-TYPE PRESS

CONTENTS

5

ΠΕΡΙΕΧΟΜΕΝΑ

INTRODUCTION

Modern Greek is not nearly so difficult as it looks. So many of the thousands of tourists who visit Greece take one look at the Greek alphabet and say "not for me"; this is a great pity, because they could so easily learn enough to make the incomprehensible wording on shops and placards come alive and mean something to them, and enough to be able to exchange real greetings and remarks with Greeks. True, it is possible to see the sights and lie on the beach without knowing a word of Greek, and in Athens and other large towns the shops and restaurants that deal with tourists usually speak English, but you can't rely on finding people who speak English everywhere: even in the cheaper restaurants and tavernas in Athens, and in most of the shops off the main streets, people seldom speak anything but Greek, while, with the possible exception of Customs officers and Tourist Police, it is rare to find a minor official anywhere who knows English. So if you should need the help of a Gendarme in the country, if you should want to give clear instructions in a garage, or buy something in a street-market or say anything to a maid in a hotel—in fact if you want to do anything more than sit in a motor-coach and be shepherded around the ruins—a few words of Greek are essential.

Your first problem is to learn the alphabet; this should not take more than an hour, yet once you have learnt it, Greek becomes little more outlandish than German or Italian. The pronunciation is straightforward, though words tend to be long. The vocabulary is not particularly reminiscent of English, though it contains many words internationally current and useful to tourists, while others will be familiar in scientific contexts. Greek grammar is much more complicated than English grammar, and no attempt is made to teach it in this book. The phrases that follow are all grammatically correct as they stand, but if you substitute other words you are likely to make mistakes. However, correctness isn't everything, and you will probably be understood. Use single words or short phrases as far as possible, articulate clearly, make liberal use of gestures and if necessary show the word or phrase in the book.

ALPHABET AND PRONUNCIATION

The spelling of a Greek word shows its pronunciation, though as certain sounds may be spelt in more than one way, pronunciation is not a sure guide to spelling. In this book every Greek word is written both in

11

Greek and in English letters giving an approximation to the Greek sound. In order to be understood you should speak slowly and loudly, articulating each consonant clearly. Remember two very important rules:

(1) *Keep the vowel sounds pure*; for example, the word τό, "the", does *not* rhyme with English "go", but is pronounced like "tot" without the final "t".

(2) *Put the stress firmly on the accented syllable.* Printed Greek has three kinds of accent—ά, ὰ, ᾶ—but all you have to know is that you stress the syllable the accent is on. For example, πότε (póte) means "when?", but ποτέ (poté) means "never". There are many such distinctions depending entirely upon which syllable is stressed.

N.B. *Do not confuse the "breathings" with stressed accents. These breathings are little commas that go over initial vowels—ὁ, ὀ—and have no connection with stress.*

The Greek sounds and spelling and the English renderings to be used in this book follow.

Vowels

There are five vowel sounds in Greek. There is no exact English equivalent to any of them, but you will do well enough if you keep them pure, as recommended above, and do not let them become diphthongs.

English rendering	Pronunciation	Greek spelling, in capital and small letters
a	between the "a" in "man" and that in "father"	A, α
e	like "e" in "men", but often longer	E, ε. AI, αι
i	like "ee" in "meet"	I, ι. H, η. Y, υ. EI, ει. OI, οι. YI, υι
o	roughly as in "on", but with the lips well rounded	O, o. Ω, ω
oo	roughly as in moon. Lips well rounded	OY, ου

You will notice that certain sounds, and especially the sound "i", can be indicated by a variety of letters.

Diphthongs

These are sounds that start as one vowel and change to another, as in English "boy", "day", "sky". In Greek, diphthongs are comparatively rare:

ai	roughly as in "eye"	AÏ, αϊ. AH, αη
au	roughly as in "cow"	AOY, αου
ei	roughly as in "day"	EÏ, εϊ
oi	roughly as in "boy"	OÏ, οϊ. OH, οη

Note that the above refers only to *sounds*. Two vowels often appear together in Greek spelling, but usually make only one vowel-*sound*.

Vowel combinations

The Greek letter υ, following α, ε or η, is pronounced as "f" or "v", thus:

αυ	before a vowel or voiced consonant makes "av"
αυ	before an unvoiced consonant makes "af"
ευ	before a vowel or voiced consonant makes "ev"
ευ	before an unvoiced consonant makes "ef"

Consonants

Greek consonant sounds are nearly all the same as English ones. The most notable exceptions are the sounds of γ and χ, which have no equivalent in English. There are also some common English sounds that in Greek are represented by combinations of letters.

Since the Greek letters representing consonant sounds are a little confusing, for ease of learning we may divide them into three categories:

(1) Letters that look like English letters and make the same sound:

K, κ
T, τ
M
N
Z

(2) Letters that look like English letters but make a different sound:

B, β	makes "v"
P, ρ	makes "r"
X, χ	makes (i) before a, o, oo, a sound like "ch" in Scottish "loch"; (ii) before i or e, a sound like the beginning of "hue" or "hear"

Note also the vowels H and Y, υ, already mentioned, which both make "i", and the vowel ω (small) which makes "o".

(3) Letters that look like no English letter.

| Γ, γ | this letter, gamma, has two sounds: before a, o, oo, ai, oi it is a guttural "g" made at the back of the throat. It |

may be learnt by pronouncing English hard "g", as in "got", and gradually relaxing the vocal chords; it is a sound which may be held, unlike "g", which is momentary. Shown in this book as "gh". Before i, e, γ has the sound of English "y" in "yet", and is shown as "y".

Δ, δ	as "th" in "**then**". Here shown as "**th**" (heavy type)
Θ, θ	as "th" in "thin". Here shown as "th" (light type)
Λ, λ	as English "l"
Ξ, ξ	as English "x". Here shown as "ks"
Π, π	as English "p"
Σ, σ, ς	as English "s". The second small one is used only at the end of a word.
Φ, φ	as English "f"
Ψ, ψ	as English "ps", pronounced thus even at the beginning of a word.
Μ, μ	as English "m"
Ν, ν	as English "n"
Η, η	as "i" (see vowels)
Ω, ω	as English "o" (see vowels)
Ζ, з	as English "z"

Combinations of consonants

ΜΠ, μπ	makes "b" as in "but" or "mb" as in "ember"
ΝΤ, ντ	makes a nasal "d" or "nd" as in "ending"
ΓΓ, γγ	makes "ng" as in "longer"
ΓΚ, γκ	makes "g" as in "got"
Σ, σ	before a voiced consonant, as "m", "n", "v", makes "z"
ΤΣ, τσ	at the beginning of a word, roughly "ch"
ΤΖ, τз	roughly "j"

For practice, try deciphering these words. They are all English names in Greek transliteration:

Σμίθ, Σκότ, Λέν, Τόμ, ῎Αλφ, Τζόν, Γκόρντον, ῎Ακτον, Βικτώρια, Τόψη, Μπόμπ, ΚΕΝΝΕΝΤΥ, ΚΟΛΛΙΝΖ, ΜΑΚΜΙΛΛΑΝ, ΛΙΒΕΡΠΟΥΛ, ΚΑΡΝΤΙΦ

Here are some easily understood Greek words with their English pronunciation:

τηλέφωνο (tiléfono); τηλεγράφημα (tileghráfima); ᾿Αμερική (Amerikí); ᾿Ιταλία (Italía); Γερμανία (Yermanía); ᾿Αγγλία (Anglía); μαθηματικά (mathimatiká); ἀσπιρίνη (aspiríni); πνευμονία (pnevmonía); ἀεροδρόμιον (aëro**th**rómion); ψυχολογία (psiholoyía)

Here is the complete Greek alphabet, in order, for reference:

Name	Capital	Small	Sound	Example	Meaning
álfa	Α	α	lark	ἄνω	(áno) upper
víta	Β	β	*v*im	βέρα	(véra) wedding-ring
gháma	Γ	γ	see notes	γάμος	(ghámos) wedding
				γελῶ	(yeló) I laugh
thélta	Δ	δ	*th*en	δέκα	(**théka**) ten
épsilon	Ε	ε	*e*gg	ἐφτά	(eftá) seven
zíta	Ζ	ʒ	*z*ip	ʒωή	(zo-í) life
íta	Η	η	m*ee*t	ἥλιος	(ílios) sun
thíta	Θ	θ	*th*in	θέλω	(thélo) I want
ióta	Ι	ι	m*ee*t	ἴσια	(ísia) straight
káppa	Κ	κ	*k*iss	κρασί	(krasí) wine
lám**tha**	Λ	λ	*l*ook	λαιμός	(lemós) neck
mí	Μ	μ	*m*ad	μικρό	(mikró) small
ní	Ν	ν	*n*ot	ναί	(né) yes
ksí	Ξ	ξ	fo*x*	ξέρω	(kséro) I know
ómikron	Ο	ο	n*o*t	ὄχι	(óhi) no
pí	Π	π	*p*ig	ποῦ	(poó) where?
ró	Ρ	ρ	*r*at	ρεῦμα	(révma) current
síghma	Σ	σ	*s*un	σκέψις	(sképsis) thought
	(before v, m, n)		*z*ip	σβύνω	(zvíno) I extinguish
táf	Τ	τ	*t*op	τρία	(tría) three
ípsilon	Υ	υ	m*ee*t	ὕφασμα	(ífazma) cloth
fí	Φ	φ	*f*ish	φεύγω	(févgho) I go
hí	Χ	χ	see notes	χάνω	(háno) I lose
				χέρι	(héri) hand
psí	Ψ	ψ	co*ps*e	ψητό	(psitó) roast
omégha	Ω	ω	n*o*t	ὥρα	(óra) hour

NOTE ON PHONETIC RENDERINGS

Throughout this book Greek words are given in the Greek alphabet and spelling, followed by an approximate phonetic rendering in English letters. Please remember that the English version is only approximate, and that English sounds cannot possibly produce a Greek word; indeed, certain renderings, such as "héri" for χέρι or "eghó" for ἐγώ, cannot be correctly read without reference to the notes on pronunciation. Perfect consistency in the English renderings has been sacrificed in order to avoid misreadings: e.g. σχάρας is rendered as "skháras" rather than "sháras" and ποῖος as "pyós" instead of "piós".

Certain words in Greek, notably possessive adjectives, are pronounced as if they were part of the preceding word, and are here written as one with that word, e.g. τό παλτό μου (my overcoat) τό paltómoo.

Stress is indicated by an accent over the stressed syllable, as in Greek.

GRAMMAR

Greek grammar is complicated by the fact that pronouns, nouns and adjectives change their endings according to their function in the sentence, according to whether they are singular or plural and according to whether they are masculine, feminine or neuter. Verbs, too, change their endings according to person and number, and often change radically with the tense. The articles, which are more often used than in English, have many different forms—indeed, there are twelve different ways of writing "the" in everyday Greek. Thus for most words it is impossible to give a single translation that will fit all possible sentences.

Instead, the endings of a demonstrative pronoun and an adjective are given. All pronouns and adjectives follow this pattern:

The pronoun αὐτός (aftós) "this"

SINGULAR	Masculine		Feminine		Neuter	
Subject:	αὐτός	(aftós)	αὐτή	(aftí)	αὐτό	(aftó)
Possessive:	αὐτοῦ	(aftoó)	αὐτῆς	(aftís)	αὐτοῦ	(aftoó)
Object:	αὐτόν	(aftón)	αὐτήν	(aftín)	αὐτό	(aftó)
PLURAL						
Subject:	αὐτοί	(afti)	αὐτές	(aftés)	αὐτά	(aftá)
Possessive:	αὐτῶν	(aftón)	αὐτῶν	(aftón)	αὐτῶν	(aftón)
Object:	αὐτούς	(aftoós)	αὐτές	(aftés)	αὐτά	(aftá)

The adjective καλός (kalós) "good"

SINGULAR	Masculine		Feminine		Neuter	
Subject:	καλός	(kalós)	καλή	(kalí)	καλό	(kaló)
Possessive:	καλοῦ	(kaloó)	καλῆς	(kalís)	καλοῦ	(kaloó)
Object:	καλό	(kaló)	καλή	(kalí)	καλό	(kaló)
PLURAL						
Subject:	καλοί	(kalí)	καλές	(kalés)	καλά	(kalá)
Possessive:	καλῶν	(kalón)	καλῶν	(kalón)	καλῶν	(kalón)
Object:	καλούς	(kaloós)	καλές	(kalés)	καλά	(kalá)

There is also a form "καλέ" (kalé) often used in addressing people; it is colloquial and is perhaps the equivalent of English "mate".

Compare these sentences

He is a good man.   Αὐτός εἶναι καλός ἄνθρωπος (aftós íne kalós ánthropos).
She is a good woman.   Αὐτή εἶναι καλή γυναῖκα (aftí íne kalí yinéka).
This is a good child.   Αὐτό εἶναι καλό παιδί (aftó íne kaló pethí).

This is the house of the good man.   Αὐτό εἶναι τό σπίτι τοῦ καλοῦ ἀνθρώπου
(aftó íne tó spíti toó kaloó anthrópoo).

These tables may be of help if you wish to indicate something; by study-
ing them you will be able to avoid saying "him" when you mean "her",
or "is it good?" when you mean "are they good?".   You will, of course,
find it difficult to remember the gender of nouns, which you should
know in order to give their adjectives the correct endings; unfortunately
there is no easy way to tell the gender, which has little or no connection
with the sex of the thing in question and which is seldom apparent from
the ending of the word.   Thus ὁ δρόμος (ó thrómos) the road, ὁ ἄνδρας
(ó ánthras) the man, are masculine, but ἡ ὁδός (í othós) the street,
ἡ κοπέλλα (í kopéla) the girl, are feminine and τό κράτος (tó krátos) the
state, τό κορίτσι (tó korítsi) the girl, are neuter.   In fact the easiest
way to tell the gender of a noun is from its article.   Accordingly the
declensions of the nouns are not given here, but the definite article,
"the", is fully declined below.

SINGULAR	*Masculine*		*Feminine*		*Neuter*	
Subject:	ὁ	(o)	ἡ	(i)	τό	(to)
Possessive:	τοῦ	(too)	τῆς	(tis)	τοῦ	(too)
Object:	τό (ν)	(to(n)	τή (ν)	(ti(n)	τό	(to)
PLURAL						
Subject:	οἱ	(i)	οἱ	(i)	τά	(ta)
Possessive:	τῶν	(ton)	τῶν	(ton)	τῶν	(ton)
Object:	τούς	(toos)	τίς	(tis)	τά	(ta)

Throughout this book all Greek nouns are given with their articles
(singular subject-form: ὁ, ἡ, τό) to help you identify their gender.
     Verbs are a bit easier to handle than nouns.   They change their
endings according to their grammatical subjects (I, you, he, etc.) and
all verbs in the present tense keep more or less to one of two patterns.
Below are given the present and past tenses of "to be" (irregular) and
"to have".

I am, ἐγώ εἶμαι (eghó íme)
You are (singular), ἐσύ εἶσαι (esí íse)
He is, αὐτός εἶναι (aftós íne)
She is, αὐτή εἶναι (aftí íne)
It is, αὐτό εἶναι (aftó íne)
We are, ἐμεῖς εἴμαστε (emís ímaste)
You are (plural), ἐσεῖς εἶστε (esís íste)
They are (m.) αὐτοί εἶναι (aftí íne)
            (f.) αὐτές εἶναι (aftés íne)
            (n.) αὐτά εἶναι (aftá íne)

I was	ἐγώ ἤμουνα (eghó ímoona)
You were	ἐσύ ἤσουνα (esí ísoona)
He was	αὐτός ἤτανε (aftós ítane)
We were	ἐμεῖς εἴμαστε (emís ímaste)
You were	ἐσεῖς εἴσαστε (esís ísaste)
They were	αὐτοί ἤτανε (aftí ítane)

(although pronouns have been added here, the verb-endings themselves show person, and so a pronoun subject is unnecessary before a Greek verb and is normally not used)

I have	ἔχω (ého)		I had	εἶχα (íha)
You have	ἔχεις (éhis)		You had	εἶχες (íhes)
He has	ἔχει (éhi)		He had	εἶχε (íhe)
We have	ἔχομε (éhome)		We had	εἴχαμε (íhame)
You have	ἔχετε (éhete)		You had	εἴχατε (íhate)
They have	ἔχουν (éhoon)		They had	εἶχαν (íhan)

In the *present* tense the following useful verbs have the same endings as ἔχω:

βάζω (vázo—to put), δίνω (**th**íno—to give), θέλω (thélo—to want), μπορῶ (boró—can), ξέρω (kséro—to know), παίρνω (pérno—to take), πηγαίνω (piyéno—to go)

Another very common verb is πρέπει (prépi), meaning "must", which does not change its ending at all in the present.

A sentence is made *negative* by putting δέν (**th**én) immediately before the verb, e.g. δέν ξέρω (**th**én kséro—I don't know). There is no way of indicating a *question* except by making the voice go up in pitch at the end of the sentence. (In writing you use a question mark that looks like the English semi-colon (;).) It is important to remember that at the end even of long interrogative sentences the last word must be given this decided rising inflection.

The future tense is made by adding θά (thá) immediately before the verb: θά πάω (thá páo—I shall go), δέν θά πάω (**th**én thá páo—I shall not go).

The foregoing notes on grammar are not intended to be an adequate survey of the subject, but merely a partial explanation of some features which might otherwise puzzle the user of this phrase-book. If it all looks too complicated, then stick to the words and phrases in the book.

COMMON WORDS AND PHRASES
VOCABULARY

how? πῶς; (pós)
how many? πόσα; (pósa)
how much? πόσο; (póso)
what? τί; (tí)
when? πότε; (póte)
where? ποῦ; (poó)
which? ποιό; (pyó)
who? ποιός, ποιά; (pyós, pyá)
why? γιατί; (yatí)

all, ὅλοι, ὅλες, ὅλα (óli, óles, óla) (m. f. n. plural)
all, ὅλος, ὅλη, ὅλο (ólos, óli, ólo) (m. f. n. sing.)
almost, σχεδόν (skhethón)
enough, ἀρκετά (arketá)
everybody, ὅλοι (óli)
everything, ὅλα (óla)
everywhere, παντοῦ (pandoó)
less, λιγώτερο (lighótero)
little, λίγο (lígho)
many, πολλοί, πολλές, πολλά (polí, polés, polá)
more, περισσότερο (perisótero)
much, very, πολύ (polí)
somebody, κάποιος (kápyos)
something, κάτι (káti)
nobody, κανείς (kanís)
nothing, τίποτα (típota)
nowhere, πουθενά (poothená)
never, ποτέ (poté)
too many, πάρα πολλά (párapolá)
too much, πάρα πολύ (párapolí)

above, ἐπάνω (epáno)
after, μετά (metá)
against, ἔναντι (énandi)
among, μεταξύ (metaksí)
before, (time) πρίν (prín)
before, (position) μπροστά (brostá)
behind, πίσω (píso)
below, κάτω (káto)
beside, δίπλα (thípla)
between, μεταξύ (metaksí)
elsewhere, ἀλλοῦ (aloó)

except, ἐκτός, πλήν (ektós, plín)
far, μακρυά (makryá)
for, γιά (yá)
here, ἐδῶ (ethó)
in, into, μέσα (mésa)
inside, μέσα (mésa)
left, ἀριστερά (aristerá)
near, κοντά (kondá)
on, εἰς (ís)
outside ἔξω (ékso)
over there, ἐκεῖ πέρα (ekí péra)
right, δεξιά (theksyá)
there, ἐκεῖ (ekí)
through, διά μέσου (thyá mésoo)
towards, πρός (prós)
until, μέχρι (méhri)
without, χωρίς (horís)
with, μέ (mé)

N.B. *Many spatial relationships can be indicated by* εἰς (ís) *with the appropriate article, often assimilated thus:* στό, στή, στά, στούς (stó, stí, stá, stoós) *This can mean "at", "on", "in".*

MINIMUM GREEK

Try to learn the words under this heading by heart.   They will carry you a long way.

For greeting or parting, at any time of the day.   χαίρετε (hérete)

Please.   παρακαλῶ (parakaló)
(*also useful if you do not understand something, to be said then with rising, interrogative, intonation, and also to attract attention*)

Thank you.   εὐχαριστῶ (efharistó)
(*the answer to thank you is "please" again, like German "bitte"*)

Yes.   ναί (né)
No, not. (*before nouns, pronouns, adjectives*) ὄχι (óhi)
        (*to make negative of verbs*) δέν (thén)
Slowly! gently! carefully! (*very useful word*) σιγά (sighá)
This (*or "that", useful when indicating an object*) αὐτό (aftó)
Don't! μή (mí!)
How much does it cost? πόσο κάνει; (póso káni?)
Where is (it)? ποῦ εἶναι; (poó íne?)
I want . . . θέλω (thélo)
I haven't got . . . δέν ἔχω (théného)
All right, o.k., suitable, in order ἐντάξει (endáksi)
very, a lot, much, too much πολύ (polí)
a little λίγο (lígho)
big μεγάλο (meghálo)
small μικρό (mikró)

Lastly, an ubiquitous word, ὁρίστε (oríste), *that can mean, depending on the situation,* "**here you are**" *(offering something),* or "**hey**" *(to attract attention),* or "**hallo**" *(answering the phone),* or "**what can I do for you?**", *or even* "**what on earth is going on here!**" *(but this demands an intonation that only a Greek had better attempt)*

POLITE EXPRESSIONS

Greek has considerably more set expressions for particular occasions than has English. The English exchange "please"—"thank you", for example, has in Greek three parts: **Please—thank you—please,** παρακαλῶ, εὐχαριστῶ, παρακαλῶ (parakaló—efharistó—parakaló). There are elaborate phrases for welcoming a guest, congratulating people on sundry events, to be repeated at meal times, at parting and so forth. They are well worth learning, as they give a great impression of goodwill.

Welcome

> καλῶς ἤρθατε (kalós írthate)
> καλῶς ὁρίσατε (kalós orísate)

to which the correct reply is:

> καλῶς σᾶς βρήκαμε (kalós sás vríkame)

Rather more casual is καλόστονε (kalóstone), "**welcome**", while the phrases γειά σας, γειά σου (yásas, yásoo) or simply γειά (yá), which mean "**health to you**", rather like "**hail**" in English, are very common, but they imply some degree of familiarity.

Address

In Greek the second person singular, English "thou", is much used. Most of the phrases in this book addressed to a second person are written in the plural, because they will probably be used to adult strangers. However, if you talk to a child you should certainly use the singular. Again, in the country, peasants nearly always use the singular. If you make any Greek friends, notice which they use to you and follow suit; since the plural sounds very cold, and most Greeks hate to seem cold, the chances are they will use the singular. Remember that the usual second person singular verb ending is "-is", "-as", instead of "-ete", "-ate" for the plural.

When addressing someone for the first time, or attracting his attention, say κύριε (kírie), κυρία (kiría), δεσποινίς (thespinís)—**Mr., Mrs., Miss.** These titles may be used with or without the name, like French "monsieur". When referring to someone, use the subject form κύριος (kírios), κυρία (kiría), δεσποινίς (thespinís), or the object form κύριο (kírio), κυρία (kiría), δεσποινίδα (thespinítha). Note that it is quite common to use κύριος, etc., with the *Christian* name, as κύριος Γιάννης, κυρία Ἕλλη (kírios yánis, kiría Éli)—**Mr. John, Mrs. Elli.** Priests should be addressed as πάτερ (páter).

Parting

'Αντίο (andío)
Χαίρετε (hérete) } says the one leaving,

to which the answer is στό καλό (stó kaló) from the one remaining. If the other is going on a long journey, καλό ταξίδι (kaló taksíthi)—**bon voyage**—is appropriate.

Congratulations

Greeks do not celebrate their birthdays, but their name-days—the day of the saint after whom they are named. (This, by the way, makes for great congestion on the roads and in buses on any popular saint's day, because everyone is out on a round of visits to friends bearing the name in question.) Meeting someone on his name-day and also at Christmas, the New Year and Easter, you say Χρόνια Πολλά (hrónia pollá), lit. "**many years**". The answer except on name days is 'Επίσης (epísis)—"**and to you too**".

Another wish used at birthdays, weddings and name-days is Νά ζήσετε (ná zísate)—"**may you live**" and at christenings Νά σᾶς ζήση (ná sás zísi)—"**may** (the child) **live for you**". This last wish is also appropriate when anyone tells you about or shows you photographs of his child.

To congratulate someone on an achievement, say Μπράβο (brávo), or, more formally, συγχαρητήρια (sinhariúria).

Before eating and when parting from someone before a meal time, you may say καλή ὄρεξη (kalí óreksi)—"**good appetite**".

To someone who appears in a new dress, shoes, etc., say Μέ γειά (meyá—lit. "**wear it in good health**"). This is almost obligatory.

When drinking, the equivalent of "**cheers**" is εἰς ὑγείαν (is iyían) or γειά σας (ya sas).

To someone who is ill, say περαστικά (perastiká)—"**get well**".

When introduced to someone, say χαίρω πολύ (héro polí)—"**pleased to meet you**" and on leaving this new acquaintance, χάρηκα πολύ (hárika polí), "**pleased to have met you**".

Good morning.	Καλημέρα.
	kaliméra
Good evening.	Καλησπέρα.
	kalispéra
Good day or **good-bye.**	Χαίρετε.
	hérete
Please. Thank you.	Παρακαλῶ. Εὐχαριστῶ.
	parakaló. efharistó
Yes. No.	Ναί. Ὄχι.
	né. óhi

N.B. *The word* ὄχι, **no**, *is often accompanied by an upward tilting of the face or a momentary raising of the eyebrows, together with a click of the tongue. This gesture may altogether replace the word, like a shake of the head in England, and has often puzzled the uninitiated.*

I beg your pardon. (*as an apology*)	Παρντόν. parndón
	Συγνώμη. sighnómi
	Μέ συγχωρεῖτε. mé sinhoríte
I beg your pardon. (*I didn't hear you*)	Ὁρίστε; oríste?
Please sit down.	Καθῆστε παρακαλῶ. kathíste, parakaló
Can I help you?	Μπορῶ νά σᾶς βοηθήσω; boró ná sás voithíso?
How are you?	Τί κάνετε; tí kánete?
Very well—and you?	Καλά—καί σεῖς; kalá—ké sís?
How do you do.	Χαίρω πολύ. héro polí
Am I disturbing you?	Σᾶς ἐνοχλῶ; sás enohló?
It doesn't matter (to me).	Δέν (μέ) πειράζει. thén (mé) pirázi
I am terribly sorry.	Λυποῦμαι πολύ. lipoóme polí
Just a minute.	Μιά στιγμή. miá stighmí
Thank you for your hospitality.	Σᾶς εὐχαριστῶ γιά τήν φιλοξενία σας. sás efharistó yá tín filokseníasas
We had a very good time.	Περάσαμε ὡραῖα. perásame oréa

Enjoy yourself.   Καλή διασκέδαση.
                             kalí thiaskéthasi

After you. (*for urging some-*   Περᾶστε, παρακαλῶ.
one to enter ahead of you; also
means "**come in**")
                             peráste, parakaló

MISCELLANEOUS EXPRESSIONS

Because. Because of.   Γιατί. Διότι
                             yatí. thióti

That's it.   Αὐτό εἶναι.
                             aftó íne

Too much. Too dear.   Πολύ. Πολύ ἀκριβό.
                             polí. polí akrivó

Very cheap.   Πολύ φθηνό.
                             polí fthinó

Quickly. Slowly.   Γρήγορα. Σιγά.
                             ghríghora. sighá

Gently.   Σιγά—σιγά.
                             sighá sighá

Look out!   Προσέχετε!
                             proséhete!

Come in.   'Εμπρός. Περᾶστε.
                             embrós. peráste

Go out.   Βγῆτε ἔξω.
                             vyíte ékso

This way. That way.   'Απ'ἐδῶ. 'Απ 'ἐκεῖ.
                             ap ethó. ap ekí

I am an Englishman.   Εἶμαι Ἄγγλος.
                             íme ánghlos

I am an Englishwoman.   Εἶμαι 'Αγγλίδα.
                             íme anghlítha

What is the matter?   Τί συμβαίνει;
                             tí simvéni?

I don't know.	Δέν ξέρω. thén kséro
You are right.	Ἔχετε δίκαιο. éhete thíkeo
You are wrong.	Δέν ἔχετε δίκαιο. thén éhete thíkeo
This doesn't work.	Αὐτό δέν δουλεύει. aftó thén thoolévi
On the contrary.	Ἀντιθέτως. andithétos
Not at all (*in contradiction*).	Καθόλου. kathóloo
Wonderful!	Θαῦμα! thávma!
How lovely!	Τί ὡραῖο! tí oréo!
I (don't) think so.	(Δέν) νομίζω. (thén) nomízo
Listen. Look.	Ἀκοῦστε. Κυττᾶξτε akoóste. kitákste
Very well.	Πολύ καλά. polí kalá
Nothing else.	Τίποτε ἄλλο. típote állo
Anything else?	Τίποτε ἄλλο; típote állo?
Whose turn is it?	Ποιανοῦ σειρά εἶναι; pianoó sirá íne?
By chance.	Τυχαία. tihéa
It is not my fault.	Δέν φταίω ἐγώ. thén ftéo eghó
I do my best.	Κάνω ὅ, τι μπορῶ. káno óti bóro
What is that?	Τί εἶναι αὐτό; tí íne aftó?

Like this.	Ἔτσι.
	étsi
I am looking for ...	Ψάχνω.
	psáhno ...
Will this do?	Κάνει αὐτό;
	káni aftó?

GENERAL DIFFICULTIES

I don't understand you.	Δέν σᾶς καταλαβαίνω.
	thén sás kataláveno
What do you want?	Τί θέλετε;
	tí thélete?
Do you speak English?	Ξέρετε Ἀγγλικά;
	ksérete anghliká?
French?	Ξέρετε Γαλλικά;
	ksérete ghaliká?
Italian?	Ξέρετε Ἰταλικά;
	ksérete italiká?
German?	Ξέρετε Γερμανικά;
	ksérete yermaniká?
I don't know Greek.	Δέν ξέρω Ἑλληνικά
	thén kséro eliniká
Please speak slowly.	Παρακαλῶ, μιλᾶτε ἀργά.
	parakaló, miláte arghá
Does anyone here know English?	Ξέρει κανένας ἐδῶ Ἀγγλικά;
	kséri kanénas ethó anghliká?
Perhaps you will find it here.	Ἴσως νά τό βρῆς ἐδῶ.
	ísos ná tó vríte ethó
Wait, I am looking for the phrase in this book.	Περιμένετε, ψάχνω τή φράση σ'αὐτό τό βιβλίο.
	periménete, psáhno tí frási saftó tó vivlío
Please read this.	Διαβάστε αὐτό, παρακαλῶ.
	thiaváste aftó, parakaló

Where are we going?	Πού πᾶμε; poó páme?
Where are you going?	Πού πᾶτε; poó páte?
Come quickly and see . . .	Ἐλᾶτε γρήγορα νά δῆτε . . . eláte ghríghora ná thíte . .
My bag has been stolen.	Μοῦ κλέψανε τήν τσάντα. moó klépsane tin tzánda
That man is following me everywhere.	Αὐτός μέ παρακολουθεῖ παντοῦ. aftós mé parakoloothí pandoó
I shall call a policeman.	Θά φωνάξω τόν ἀστυφύλακα. thá fonákso tón astifílaka
I shall stay here.	Θά μείνω ἐδῶ. thá míno ethó
Will you help me?	Θέλετε νά μέ βοηθήσετε; thélete ná mé voithísate?
Help! Fire! Thief!	Βοήθεια! Φωτιά! Κλέφτης! vo-íthya! fotyá! kléftis!
Beware.	Προσοχή. prosohí
Who are you?	Ποιός, ποιά εἶστε; pyós(m.) pyá(f.) íste?
I don't know you.	Δέν σᾶς ξέρω. thén sás kséro
I don't want to speak to you.	Δέν θέλω νά σᾶς μιλήσω. thén thélo ná sás milíso
Leave me alone.	Ἀφῆστε με. afísteme
Go away.	Φύγετε. fíyete
That will do!	Φτάνει πιά. ftáni pyá
You are mistaken.	Κάνετε λάθος. kánete láthos
I didn't do it.	Δέν τό ἔκανα ἐγώ. thén tó ékana eghó

I will give you nothing.   Δέν θά σᾶς δώσω τίποτα.
thén thá sás thóso típota

It is very annoying.   Εἶναι πολύ ἐνοχλητικό.
íne polí enohlitikó

It has nothing to do with me.   Δέν μέ ἀφορᾶ.
thén mé aforá

Where should one apply?   Ποῦ νά ρωτήσω;
poó ná rotíso?

What does that mean?   Τί θά πεῖ αὐτό;
tí thá pí aftó?

What must I do?   Τί πρέπει νά κάνω;
tí prépi ná káno?

Where can I find . . . ?   Ποῦ μπορῶ νά βρῶ . . ;
poó boró ná vró . . .?

What have I done?   Τί ἔκανα;
tí ékana?

I have done nothing.   Δέν ἔκανα τίποτα.
thén ékana típota

I have paid you.   Σᾶς ἔχω πληρώσει.
sás ého plirósi

I have paid you enough.   Σᾶς πλήρωσα ἀρκετά.
sás plírosa arketá

Let me pass.   ᾽Αφῆστε με νά περάσω.
afístete ná peráso

Where is the British Con-   Ποῦ εἶναι τό Βρεττανικό
sulate?   Προξενεῖο;
poó íne tó vretanikó proksenío?

PUBLIC NOTICES

ΕΙΣΟΔΟΣ, ΕΞΟΔΟΣ (ísothos, éksothos) = **Entrance, Exit**
ΑΠΑΓΟΡΕΥΕΤΑΙ (apaghorévete) = **Forbidden**
ΕΝΟΙΚΙΑΖΕΤΑΙ (enikiázete) **To Let**
ΠΩΛΕΙΤΑΙ (políte) = **For Sale**
ΣΤΑΣΙΣ (stásis) = **Bus Stop**

ΠΡΟΣΟΧΗ ΧΡΩΜΑΤΑ (prosohí hrómata) = **Wet Paint**
ΩΘΗΣΑΤΕ, ΣΥΡΑΤΕ (othísate, sírate) = **Push, Pull**
ΚΙΝΔΥΝΟΣ (kínthinos) = **Danger**
ΑΝΟΙΚΤΟΝ, ΚΛΕΙΣΤΟΝ (aniktón, klistón) = **Open, Closed**
ΔΙΑΝΥΚΤΕΡΕΥΕΙ (thianikterévi) = **Open All Night**
ΓΥΝΑΙΚΩΝ, ΑΝΔΡΩΝ (yinekón, anthrón) = **Ladies, Gentle-
men**
ΕΔΩ ΤΗΛΕΦΩΝΕΙΤΕ (ethó tilefoníte) = **Telephone Here**
ΤΗΛΕΦΩΝΟ ΔΙΑ ΤΟ ΚΟΙΝΟ (tiléfono thiá tó kinó) = **Public
Telephone**
ΕΙΣΟΔΟΣ ΕΛΕΥΘΕΡΑ (ísothos elefthéra) = **Entrance Free**
ΙΣΟΓΕΙΟΝ (isóyion) = **Ground Floor**
ΥΠΟΓΕΙΟΝ (ipóyion) = **Basement**

TIME

VOCABULARY

after, μετά (metá)
afternoon, τό ἀπόγευμα (tó apóyevma)
always, πάντοτε (pándote)
at once, ἀμέσως (amésos)
beginning, ἡ ἀρχή (í arhí)
calendar, τό ἡμερολόγιον (tó imerolóyon)
clock, τό ρολόϊ (tó rolóy)
day, ἡμέρα (i méra)
during, κατά (katá)
early, νωρίς (norís)
end, τό τέλος (tó télos)
evening, τό βράδυ (tó **vráthi**)
first πρῶτος (prótos)
fortnight, τό δεκαπενθήμερον (to **th**ekapenthímeron)
hour, ἡ ὥρα (i óra)
last, τελευταῖος (teleftéos)
late, (adverb), ἀργά (arghá)
midday, τό μεσημέρι (tó mesiméri)
middle, ἡ μέση (i mési)
midnight, τά μεσάνυχτα (tá mesánihta)
month, ὁ μήνας (ó mínas)
morning, τό πρωί (tó proí)
never, ποτέ (poté)
next day, ἡ ἄλλη μέρα (í álli méra)
night, ἡ νύχτα (í níhta)
now, τώρα (tóra)

often, συχνά (sihná)
sometimes, μερικές φορές (merikés forés)
soon, σέ λίγο (sé lígho)
then, τότε (tóte)
today, σήμερα (símera)
tomorrow, αὔριο (ávrio)
week, ἡ ἑβδομάδα (i evthomátha)
watch, τό ρολόϊ (tó rolói)
year, τό ἔτος (tó étos)
yesterday, χθές (hthés)

CLOCK TIME

What time is it?   Τί ὥρα εἶναι;
                                    tí óra íne?

It is late, early   Εἶναι ἀργά, νωρίς.
                                    íne arghá, norís

It is one o'clock, two, three, Εἶναι μία ἡ ὥρα, δύο ἡ ὥρα,
etc.   τρεῖς ἡ ὥρα.
                                    íne mía í óra, **thío** í óra, trís í óra

It is five past one.   Εἶναι μία καί πέντε.
                                    íne mía ké pénde

It is a quarter past three.   Εἶναι τρεῖς καί τέταρτο.
                                    íne trís ké tétarto

It is half past four.   Εἶναι τέσσερις καί μισή.
                                    íne tésseris ké misí

It is twenty to six.   Εἶναι ἕξη παρά εἴκοσι.
                                    íne éksi pará íkosi

It is a quarter to six.   Εἶναι ἕξη παρά τέταρτο.
                                    íne éksi pará tétarto

It is noon, midnight.   Εἶναι μεσημέρι, μεσάνυχτα.
                                    íne mesiméri, mesánihta

Three o'clock in the morn-   Τρεῖς τό πρωΐ.
ing.
                                    trís tó pro-í

Six o'clock in the evening.   Ἕξη τό ἀπόγευμα.
                                    éksi tó apóyevma

Three o'clock in the after-   Τρεῖς τό ἀπόγευμα.
noon.

                    tris tó apógevma

It is exactly seven.   Εἶναι ἑπτά ἀκριβῶς.
                    íne eptá akrivós

My watch is slow (fast). Τό ρολόϊ μου πάει πίσω,
                          μπροστά.
           tó rolóimoo pái píso, brostá

You have plenty of time. Ἔχετε πολύ καιρό.
                    éhete polí keró

I have no time.   Δέν ἔχω καιρό.
                  thén ého keró

It's time we left.   Εἶναι ὥρα νά φύγουμε.
                íne óra ná fighoome

Take your time.   Μέ τήν ἡσυχία σου.
                 mé tín isihíasoo

We are in a hurry.   Βιαζόμαστε.
             viazómaste

I am in a hurry.   Βιάζομαι.
             viázome

Hurry up.   Γρήγορα.
             ghríghora

He has come early.   Ἦρθε νωρίς.
             írthe norís

He is late.   Ἄργησε.
             áryise

Where can he be?   Ποῦ νά εἶναι;
            poó ná íne?

At last.   Ἐπί τέλους.
            epí téloos

At the latest.   Τό ἀργότερο.
            tó arghótero

How long does it take? Πόσο καιρό κάνει;
            póso keró káni?

DAYS OF THE WEEK

Sunday, Ἡ Κυριακή (i kiriakí)
Monday, Ἡ Δευτέρα (i theftéra)
Tuesday, Ἡ Τρίτη (i tríti)
Wednesday, Ἡ Τετάρτη (i tetárti)
Thursday, Ἡ Πέμπτη (i pémpti)
Friday, Ἡ Παρασκευή (i paraskeví)
Saturday, Τό Σάββατο (tó sávato)

During the day.	Τήν ἡμέρα.
	tin iméra
At night.	Τή νύχτα.
	ti níhta
This evening.	Ἀπόψε.
	apópse
Last night, yesterday morning.	Χθές τό βράδυ, χθές τό πρωΐ.
	hthés to vráthi, hthés to proí
Tomorrow morning.	Αὔριο πρωΐ.
	ávrio proí
The day after tomorrow.	Μεθαύριο.
	methávrio
The day before yesterday.	Προχθές.
	prohthés
Every day.	Κάθε μέρα.
	káthe méra
Daily.	Καθημερινῶς.
	kathímerinós
All day.	Ὅλη τήν ἡμέρα.
	óli tín iméra
Day and night.	Μερόνυχτα.
	merónihta
Last (next) week.	Τήν περασμένη (τήν ἄλλη) ἑβδομάδα.
	tín perazméni, tín álli, evthomátha
Last (next) Monday.	Τήν περασμένη (τήν ἄλλη) Δευτέρα.
	tín perazméni (tín álli) theftéra

A week today.	Σήμερα ὀκτώ.
	símera októ
A week ago.	Πρίν μία ἑβδομάδα.
	prín mía evthomátha
A holiday.	Γιορτή, ἀργία.
	yortí, aryía
A half-holiday.	Ἡμιαργία.
	imiaryía
A working day.	Μία ἐργάσιμη ἡμέρα.
	mía erghásimi iméra
Easter. Whitsun.	Τό Πάσχα. Ἡ Πεντηκοστή.
	tó páskha. i pendékostí
Christmas. New Year's	Τά Χριστούγεννα. Ἡ Πρωτο-
Day.	χρονιά.
	ta hristoóyenna. i protohronyá
Saint ——'s Day.	Τοῦ Ἁγίου ...
	Τῆς Ἁγίας ...
	toó ayíoo —— tís ayías ——

MONTHS AND SEASONS

January, Ἰανουάριος (yanooários)
February, Φεβρουάριος (fevrooários)
March, Μάρτιος (mártios)
April, Ἀπρίλιος (aprílios)
May, Μάϊος (máyos)
June, Ἰούνιος (ioónios)
July, Ἰούλιος (ioólios)
August, Αὔγουστος (ávghoostos)
September, Σεπτέμβριος (septémvrios)
October, Ὀκτώβριος (októvrios)
November, Νοέμβριος (noémvrios)
December, Δεκέμβριος (thekémvrios)

spring, ἡ ἄνοιξις (i ániksis)
summer, τό καλοκαίρι (to kalokéri)
autumn, τό φθινόπωρο (to fthinóporo)
winter, ὁ χειμῶνας (o himónas)

June 1st.   April 30th.   March   Ἰη Ἰουνίου.   30η Ἀπριλίου.
25th.   25η Μαρτίου.

próti ioonίoo.   triánda aprilίoo ίkosi pénde martίoo

How long have you been   Πόσο καιρό εἶστε ἐδῶ;
here?

póso keró íste ethó?

I have been here a month.   Εἶμαι ἐδῶ ἕνα μῆνα.

íme ethó éna mína

I haven't done this for a long   Ἔχω πολύ καιρό νά κάνω
time.   αὐτό.

ého polí keró ná káno aftó

FOOD, DRINK AND RESTAURANTS

Breakfast tends to be a lighter meal than in England. Lunch, at one o'clock, two o'clock or even later, is a substantial meal, as is dinner, which may be taken very late, at ten or eleven o'clock.

Establishments serving food are: the restaurant; the taverna, which is a restaurant with somewhat more local colour, often providing music and in summer often in the open-air; the pastry-shop, which usually serves cakes and pastries, ice-cream, perhaps savoury snacks—many of the more fashionable ones serve coffee, tea, beer and other drinks; the bar, serving drinks of all kinds; snack-bars of one kind and another, serving various sorts of pies and grilled tit-bits; the cafenion, which is a meeting place where men go to talk, play backgammon, drink Turkish coffee and read their newspapers—you will find a cafenion in even the smallest and remotest village; do not expect European coffee at a cafenion.

Prices at restaurants and tavernas are fixed by law, though they vary with the class of the place. Your bill will include the cost of what you have ordered—note that bread is a separate item—and an extra ten per cent for the waiter's tip. The waiter will normally have an assistant, who lays the table, brings water and wine, etc. and for whom a tip should be left on the table.

Menus are often printed in English or French as well as Greek at the restaurants frequented by tourists; at others, though, they are usually hand-written in Greek and consequently hard to make out. If you cannot understand what is available either by reading or asking, then ask to see what they have.

Drinks

Water. In general, water in Greece is perfectly safe to drink. The piped water supplied to towns and that from roadside and village fountains is usually excellent. If water appears to come from a well or storage tank, the tourist would be wiser to avoid it. Many sorts of bottled mineral water are available everywhere.

Coffee. Greek coffee, also called Turkish, is made of fine-ground coffee boiled with water and sugar in a special small pot—μπρίκι (bríki)—and served in very small cups with a glass of cold water. It is customary to specify the degree of sweetness required—πικρό (pikró, **bitter**), μέτριο (métrio, **medium**), γλυκό (ghlikó, **sweet**). Unless you expressly ask for another kind, Greek coffee is what you get if you order καφέ (kafé, **coffee**). *European coffee*: this may be had in some large towns in the form of (a) **French coffee** Γαλλικό καφέ (ghalikó kafé) served in a coffee-pot with a pot of hot milk. It is usually obtainable only in big hotels and fashionable cafes; (b) Espresso coffee, from Espresso bars, to be found in Athens and Salonica; (c) Instant coffee powders, known generically as Nescafé, may be found in quite remote places, though expertise in their preparation is rarer. Insist that you want **the water to boil** τό νερό νά βράζη (tó neró ná vrázi).

Tea in a teapot, with milk and sugar, may be found in big cafes and hotels in the main towns. Elsewhere it may not be served in the English way, while in villages they may proffer "**mountain tea**" τσάι τοῦ βουνοῦ (tsái toó voonoó), which is a decoction of camomile or other herbs, quite pleasant, but not tea.

Milk. Bottled milk may be had in most towns; it is good to drink, though rather thinner than English milk. Tinned milk of various kinds can be obtained everywhere and many brands of powdered milk for babies are sold in chemists'.

Wine. Retsina, a white, dry, resinated wine, is native to Attica, the region round Athens, and is what you get if you ask for κρασί (krasí, **wine**). It varies greatly in quality and in resin-strength. There are also many bottled proprietary wines worth trying. **Red** is κοκκινέλι (kokinéli) and **white** is ἄσπρο (áspro), **resinated** is ρετσίνα (retsína) and **unresinated** ἀρετσίνωτο (aretsínoto), **dry** μπροῦσκο (broósko), **sweet** γλυκό (ghlikó) and **semi-sweet** ἡμίγλυκο (imíghliko). Draught wine in a taverna is normally brought in tin measures, half a litre, μισόκιλο (misókilo), being about a pint. Alcoholic drinks may be bought and consumed at all hours.

VOCABULARY

GENERAL

ashtray, τό τασάκι (to tasáki)
assistant-waiter, ὁ μικρός (o mikrós)
bar, τό μπάρ (to bár)
bill, ὁ λογαριασμός (o loghariazmós)
bottle, ἡ μπουκάλα (i bookála)
café, τό καφενείον (to kafeníon)
chair, ἡ καρέκλα (i karékla)
coffee-pot, ἡ καφετιέρα (i kafetiéra)
cork, ὁ φελλός (o felós)
corkscrew, τό τιρμπουσόν (to tirboosón)
cup, τό φλυτζάνι (to flitzáni)
egg-cup, ἡ αὐγοθήκη (i avghothíki)
fork, τό πηρούνι (to piroóni)
glass, τό ποτήρι (to potíri)

helping, ἡ μερίδα (i merítha)
hungry, (to be), πεινάω (pináo)
knife, τό μαχαῖρι (to mahéri)
ladle, ἡ κουτάλα (i kootála)
meal, τό γεῦμα (to yévma)
menu, bill of fare, ὁ κατάλογος (o katáloghos)
milk-jug, ἡ γαλατιέρα (i ghalatyéra)
pastry-shop, τό ζαχαροπλαστεῖον (to zaharoplastíon)
plate, τό πιάτο (to piáto)
restaurant, τό ἐστιατόριο (to estiatório)
saucer, τό πιατάκι (to pyatáki)
serviette, napkin, ἡ πετσέτα (i petséta)
spoon, τό κουτάλι (to kootáli)
table, τό τραπέζι (to trapézi)
table-cloth, τό τραπεζομάντηλο (to trapezomándilo)
table-spoon, τό κουτάλι φαγητοῦ (to kootáli fayitoó)
taverna, ἡ ταβέρνα (i tavérna)
tea-pot, ἡ τσαγιέρα (i tsayéra)
teaspoon, τό κουτάλι τσαγιοῦ (to kootáli tsayoó)
thirsty (to be), διψάω (thipsáo)
tip, τό φιλοδώρημα (to filothórima)
toothpick, ἡ ὀδοντογλυφίδα (i othondoghlifítha)
waiter, τό γκαρσόν (tó garsón)
water-jug, ἡ κανάτα (í kanáta)

DRINKS

beer, ἡ μπύρα (i bíra)
brandy, τό κονιάκ (tó konyák)
chocolate, ἡ σοκολάτα (í sokoláta)
coffee, ὁ καφές (ó kafés)
    (*Greek*) ἑλληνικός (elinikós)
    (*French*) γαλλικός (ghalikós)
ice, ὁ πάγος (ó pághos)
ice-cream, τό παγωτό (tó paghotó)
lemonade (*fizzy*), ἡ γκαζόζα (í gazóza)
lemonade (*natural*), ἡ λεμονάδα χυμός (i lemonátha himós)
Mavrodaphne (*a sweet dark dessert wine*) ἡ Μαυροδάφνη
milk, τό γάλα (to ghála)
mineral water, τό μεταλλικό νερό (to metalikó neró)
orangeade (*natural*), ἡ πορτοκαλλάδα χυμός (i portokalátha himós)
orangeade (*bottled*), πορτοκαλλάδα σέ φιάλη (i portokalátha sé fyáli)
ouzo (*an aniseed-flavoured spirit*), τό οὔζο (tó oózo)
soda-water, ἡ σόδα (i sótha)
tea, τό τσάϊ (to tsái)
vissinade (*a soft drink made from cherries*), ἡ βυσσινάδα (i visinátha)
water, τό νερό (to neró)
wine, τό κρασί (to krasí)

N.B. *Savoury snacks served with beer, ouzo and other drinks are called* "**mezéthes**"
μεζέδες

FOOD

Ways of cooking:

    roast, ψητό (psitó)
    boiled, βραστό (vrastó)
    fried, τηγανιτό (tighanitó)
    grilled, τῆς σχάρας (tís skháras)
    cold, κρύο (krío)
    on the spit, τῆς σούβλας (tís soóvlas)
    baked in paper, ἐξοχικό, στό χαρτί (eksohikó, stó hartí)

Terms on the menu:

    appetizers, ὀρεκτικά (orektiká)
    soups, ἡ σοῦπες (í soópes)
    in oil, λαδερά (latherá)
    fish, ψάρια (psária)
    main dish, ἐντράδες (endráthes)
    today's special, πιάτο τῆς ἡμέρας (pyáto tís iméras)
    cooked while you wait, τῆς ὥρας (tís óras)
    salads, σαλάτες (salátes)
    fruits, φροῦτα (froóta)

General:

    apple, τό μῆλο (tó mílo)
    apricot, τό βερύκοκκο (tó veríkoko)
    artichoke, ἡ ἀγκινάρα (i anginára)
    asparagus, τά σπαράγγια (tá sparángia)
    aubergine *(egg-plant),* ἡ μελιτζάνα (i melitzána)
    banana, ἡ μπανάνα (í banána)
    beans *(haricot, in a thick soup),* τά φασόλια (tá fasólya)
    beans *(green, shredded and boiled),* φασόλια πράσινα (fasólya prásina)
    biscuit, τό μπισκότο (to biskóto)
    bread—white, brown, peasant, ψωμί—ἄσπρο—ἡμίλευκο— σταρένιο (psomí—áspro—imílefko—starénio)
    butter, τό φρέσκο βούτυρο (tó frésko voótiro)
    cabbage, τό λάχανα (tó láhana)
    cake, τό κέϊκ (tó ké-ik)
    carrot, τό καρότο (tó karóto)
    cauliflower, τό κουνουπίδι (tó koonoopíthi)
    cheese, τό τυρί (tó tirí)

      (The following are all worth trying: φέτα (féta), *a white, rather salty goat cheese;* γραβιέρα (ghravyéra), *a Cretan cheese reminiscent of Gruyere;* κασέρι (kaséri), *a crumbly yellow cheese;* μανούρι (manoóri), *a rich white soft cheese.)*

    crayfish *(called lobster),* ἀστακός (astakós)
    cream, κρέμα (kréma), γαλακτος (ghalaktos)
    cucumber, τό ἀγγούρι (tó angoóri)
    dolmathes *(meat and rice balls tightly rolled in vine or cabbage leaves),* ντολμάδες

egg, τό αὐγό (to avghó)
   fried eggs, αὐγά τηγανιτά (avghá tighanitá)
   boiled eggs, αὐγά βραστά (avghá vrastá)
   poached eggs, αὐγά ποσέ (avghá posé)
   hard-boiled eggs, αὐγά βραστά σφιχτά (avghá vrastá sfihtá)
fish, τό ψάρι (to psári)
   Some common sorts of fish to be found on menus are:
   gharíthes (**prawns**), οἱ γαρίδες (i gharíthes)
   ghlóssa (**sole**), ἡ γλῶσσα (i ghlósa)
   maríthes (*small fish like* **sprats,** *fried*), οἱ μαρίδες (i maríthes)
   barboóni (**red mullet**), τό μπαρμπούνι (to barboóni)
   sinaghrítha, ἡ συναγρίδα (i sinaghrítha)
   fagrí, τό φαγκρί (to fagrí)
   tsipoóra, ἡ τσιπούρα (i tsipoóra)
   htapóthi, (**octopus**), τό χταπόδι (to htapóthi)
   kalamarákia (*small* **squids,** *usually fried*), καλαμαράκια
   míthia (**mussels,** *usually fried*), μύδια
   héli (**freshwater eel,** *speciality of Yanina*), χέλι
   péstrofa (**trout**), πέστροφα
   Athina-ikí mayonéza *is cold fish, potatoes, carrots, covered with mayonnaise.*
   Ἀθηναϊκή μαγιονέζα
   Plakí *or* spetsopoóla *is a delicious way of preparing fish with oil,* *tomatoes,*
   onions and herbs in the oven. Πλακί, σπετσοπούλα
fruit, τό φροῦτο (tó froóto)
garlic, τό σκόρδο (tó skórtho)
grapes, τά σταφύλια (tá stafílya)
ham, τό ζαμπόν (tó zambón)
hare, ὁ λαγός (ó laghós)
ice, ὁ πάγος, (ó pághos,)
ice-cream, τό παγωτό (tó paghotó)
jam, ἡ μαρμελάδα (í marmelátha)
leek, τό πρᾶσο (tó práso)
lemon, τό λεμόνι (tó lemóni)
marmalade, ἡ μαρμελάδα νεράντζι (í marmelátha nerántzi)
meat, τό κρέας (tó kréas)
   beef, τό βωδινό (tó vothinó)
   kid, τό κατσικάκι (tó katsikaki)
   lamb, τό ἀρνί (tó arní)
   mutton, τό πρόβειο (tó próvio)
   pork, τό χοιρινό (tó hirinó)
   veal, τό μοσχάρι (to moskhári)
   steak, τό μπὸν φιλέ (tó bón filé)
   chop, ἡ μπριζόλα (í brizóla)
   sausage, τό λουκάνικο (tó lookániko)
   roast beef *is* μοσχάρι ψητό (moskhári psitó); *another dish called*
   ροσμπίφ (rozbíf) *consists of roast beef highly flavoured with garlic and*
   served with macaroni
   biftéki, μπιφτέκι, *is a grilled meat-ball made of minced beef; similar, but*
   with bread and perhaps more spice, are κεφτέδες (keftéthes) *and spicier*

still are σουτζουκάκια (sootzookákya). Yoovarlákya, γιου-βαρλάκια, *are meat-and-rice balls*

soovláki, σουβλάκι, *are small cubes of meat grilled on a skewer*

donér kebáb, ντονέρ κεμπάμπ, *consists of slices carved off a thick wedge of meat roast on a vertical spit*

melon (*sweet*), τό πεπόνι (tó pepóni)

melon (*water*), τό καρπούζι (tó karpoózi)

meze, ὁ μεζές, *savoury snacks served with drinks* (o mezés)

mint, ὁ δυόσμος (ó thyózmos)

moosakás, ὁ μουσακᾶς, *minced meat and aubergines or potatoes covered with bechamel sauce and browned in the oven*

mince, ὁ κιμᾶς (ó kimás)

mushroom, τό μανιτάρι (tó manitári)

mussels, τά μύδια (tá míthia)

mustard, ἡ μουστάρδα (í moostártha)

oil (*olive*), τό λάδι (tó láthi)

onion, τό κρεμμύδι (tó kremíthi)

orange, τό πορτοκάλλι (tó portokáli)

parsley, ὁ μαϊντανός (ó ma-indanós)

pastítsio, τό παστίτσιο, *macaroni, minced meat, browned bechamel sauce*

pastry, ἡ πάστα (í pásta) (*i.e. cream cakes, etc.*)

pastoormás, ὁ παστουρμᾶς, *heavily spiced dried or smoked meat*

peach, τό ροδάκινο (tó rothákino)

pear, τό ἀχλάδι (tó ahláthi)

peas, τά μπιζέλια (tá bizélya)

pepper, τό πιπέρι (tó pipéri)

pie, ἡ πίττα (i píta), *very popular are cheese pies, of flaky pastry and cream cheese,* τυρόπιττες (tirópites)

pilafi, τό πιλάφι (tó piláfi)

plum, τό δαμάσκηνο (tó thamáskino)

potato, ἡ πατάτα (í patáta)

poultry and game:

chicken, τό κοττόπουλο (tó kotópoolo)

duck, ἡ πάππια (í pápya)

wild duck, ἡ ἀγριόπαπια (í aghriópapya)

goose, ἡ χήνα (í hína)

partridge, ἡ πέρδικα (í pérthika)

pigeon, τό περιστέρι (tó peristéri)

turkey, ἡ γαλοπούλα (í ghalopoóla)

woodcock, ἡ μπεκάτσα (í bekátsa)

rice, τό ρύζι (tó rízi)

roll, τό κουλούρι (tó kooloóri)

salad, ἡ σαλάτα (í saláta)

salad cream (*mayonnaise*), ἡ μαγιονέζα (í mayonéza)

salami, τό σαλάμι (tó salámi)

salmon, ὁ σολωμός (ó solomós)

salt, τό ἀλάτι (tó aláti)

sauce (*or gravy*), ἡ σάλτσα (í sáltsa)

sausage, τό λουκάνικο (tó lookániko)

shrimp (or prawn), ἡ γαρίδα (í gharítha)
snail, τό σαλιγκάρι (tó salingári)
sole, ἡ γλῶσσα (í ghlóssa)
soup, ἡ σοῦπα (í soópa); there is a well-known soup thickened with egg and lemon, αὐγολέμονο (avgholémono)
soovlaki, τά σουβλάκια (tá soovlákia)
spinach, τό σπανάκι (tó spanáki)
stifátho, τό στιφάδο, stewed meat (beef or hare) with onions
strawberry, ἡ φράουλα (í fráoola)
sugar, ἡ ζάχαρη (í záhari)
taramosaláta, ἡ ταραμοσαλάτα, a paste made of fish roe, breadcrumbs, oil and sometimes onion
toast, ἡ φρυγανιά (í frighanyá)
tomato, ἡ τομάτα (í tomáta or í domáta)
vanilla, ἡ βανίλια (í vanílya)
vegetables, τά λαχανικά (tá lahaniká)
vinegar, τό ξύδι (tó ksíthi)
yoghourt, τό γιαούρτι (tó yaoórti)

Do you serve lunch (dinner)?   Σερβίρετε μεσημεριανό, (Βραδυνό);
servírete mesimerianó? vrathinó?

There are four of us.   Εἴμαστε τέσσερις.
ímaste téseris

We are together.   Εἴμαστε μαζί.
ímaste mazí

What have you got?   Τί ἔχετε;
tí éhete?

We want something light.   Θέλομε κάτι ἐλαφρό.
thélome káti elafró

We only want a snack.   Θέλομε μόνο ἕνα μεζέ.
thélome móno éna mezé

Have you got . . . ?   Ἔχετε . . .;
éhete . . .?

We are in a hurry.   Βιαζόμαστε.
viazómaste

Can you serve us at once?   Μπορεῖτ νά μᾶς σερβίρετε ἀμέσως;
boríte ná más servírete amésos?

We shall come back at one o'clock.   Θά γυρίσουμε στή μία.
thá yirísoome stí mía

We shall come back in one hour.	Θά γυρίσωμε σέ μιά ὥρα. thá yirísoome sé miá óra
Can I wash my hands?	Μπορῶ νά πλύνω τά χέρια μου; boró ná plíno tá hériamoo?
Where is the toilet?	Ποῦ εἶναι ἡ τουαλέτα; poó íne í tooaléta?
This way.	Ἀπ'ἐδῶ. ap ethó
Please bring the menu.	Παρακαλῶ, δῶστε μου τόν κατάλογο. parakaló, thóstemoo tón katálogho
What kind of soup (fish, meat) have you?	Τί σοῦπες (ψάρια, κρέας) ἔχετε; tí soópes (psária, kréas) éhete?
I will have some fried fish.	Θά πάρω τηγανιτά ψάρια. thá páro tighanitá psária
Is this nice?	Εἶναι καλό; íne kaló?
What do you serve with the roast?	Τί σερβίρετε μέ τό ψητό; tí servírete mé tó psitó?
Bring it without sauce (onions, oil).	Τό θέλω χωρίς σάλτσα (κρεμμύδια, λάδι). tó thélo horís sáltsa (kremíthya, láthi)
That cannot be done.	Αὐτό δέν γίνεται. aftó thén yínete
It's finished.	Τελείωσε. telíose
Have you finished?	Τελειώσατε; teliósate?
Would you like anything else?	Θά πάρετε τίποτα ἄλλο; thá párete típota állo?
A little more ...	Λίγο ἀκόμα ... lígho akóma ...

Waiter, bring us some bread, please.   Γκαρσόν, φέρε μας λίγο ψωμί παρακαλῶ.
garsón, féremas lígho psomí, parakaló

I would like an ice-cream, please.   Θέλω ἕνα παγωτό παρακαλῶ.
thélo éna paghotó, parakaló

What will you drink?   Τί θά πιῆτε;
tí thá pyíte?

Bring the wine now.   Φέρε τό κρασί τώρα.
fére tó krasí tóra

We do not want retsina.   Δέν θέλουμε ρετσίνα.
thén théloome retsína

I would like a glass of beer (fruit juice, lemonade).   Θέλω μία μπύρα (χυμό φρούτων, λεμονάδα)
thélo mía bíra (himó fróoton, lemonátha)

Have you anything for the child?   Ἔχετε τίποτα γιά τό παιδί;
éhete típota yá tó pethí?

Please boil some milk.   Παρακαλῶ βράστε λίγο γάλα.
parakaló, vráste lígho ghála

She does not like fizzy drinks.   Δέν τῆς ἀρέσουν τά ἀεριοῦχα ποτά.
thén tís arésoon tá aerioóha potá

Would you like some coffee?   Θέλετε καφέ;
thélete kafé?

We would like Turkish coffee, medium sweet.   Θέλουμε τούρκικο καφέ, μέτριο.
théloome toórkiko kafé, métrio

Can you make French coffee?   Φτιάχνετε γαλλικό καφέ;
ftiáhnete ghalikó kafé?

Please bring some more sugar (milk, hot water).   Φέρε, παρακαλῶ λίγη ἀκόμα ζάχαρι (γάλα, ζεστό νερό).
fére, parakaló, líyi akóma záhari (ghála, zestó neró)

Bring me some cigarettes, please.   Φέρτε μου ἕνα πακέτο τσιγάρα, παρακαλῶ.
fértemoo éna pakéto tsighára parakaló

The bill, please.	Τό λογαριασμό, παρακαλῶ.
	tó loghariazmó, parakaló
What is that for?	Γιατί εἶναι αὐτό;
	yatí íne aftó?
We had only two beers.	Πήραμε δύο ἡμπύρες μόνο.
	pírame thío bíres móno
We didn't have bread.	Δέν φάγαμε ψωμί.
	thén fághame psomí
There is a mistake in the bill.	Ὑπάρχει ἕνα λάθος στό λογα-ριασμό.
	ipárhi éna láthos stó loghariazmó
I made a mistake. I beg your pardon.	Ἔκανα λάθος. Σᾶς ζητῶ συγνώ-μη.
	ékana láthos. sás zitó sighnómi

GENERAL DIFFICULTIES

I want something very simple.	Θέλω κάτι πολύ ἁπλό.
	thélo káti polí apló
I am on a diet.	Κάνω δίαιτα.
	káno thíeta
I do not want anything with garlic (meat, fish) in it.	Δέν θέλω τίποτα μέ σκόρδο (κρέας, ψάρι).
	thén thélo típota mé skórtho (kréas, psári)
This is not fresh.	Αὐτό δέν εἶναι φρέσκο.
	aftó thén íne frésko
This does not smell very nice.	Δέν μυρίζει ὡραῖα.
	thén mirízi oréa
This has too much fat.	Ἔχει πολύ λῖπος.
	aéhi polí lípos
Without oil, (salt, sugar, gravy) please.	Χωρίς λάδι, (ἁλάτι, ζάχαρι, σάλτσα, παρακαλῶ).
	horís láthi, aláti, záhari, sáltsa, parakaló

Can I see what you have? Μπορῶ νά δῶ τί ἔχετε;
boró ná thó tí éhete?

Where can I leave the car? Ποῦ μπορῶ ν'ἀφήσω τό αὐτοκίνητο;
poó boró nafíso tó aftokínito?

I have left my glasses (my watch, my ring) in the toilet. Ἄφησα τά γυαλιά μου (τό ρολόϊ, τό δακτυλίδι) στήν τουαλέτα.

áfisa tá yalyámoo, tó rolóy, tó thaktilíthi, stín tooaléta

MOTORING

Greece may be reached by car either via Yugoslavia or by means of very well-appointed car ferries from Brindisi, in southern Italy, to Corfu and Patras.   There are also many boat services from Venice which carry cars.

To bring a car into Greece the tourist does not need an international insurance certificate (green card) as third party insurance is not compulsory. Nevertheless, it is certainly wiser to be insured, and it is compulsory in most of the countries on the way to Greece. Do not forget that British subjects need a visa to enter Yugoslavia, obtainable at Yugoslav consulates at 24 hours' notice, or at the frontier almost immediately.

Petrol, available in various grades, costs roughly the same as in Britain. All the better-known brands of petrol and oil are sold.   Service-stations and repair-shops are to be found in all towns along the main routes; in general, servicing and repairs can be done much more quickly than in Britain. Certain main routes are patrolled by yellow cars of the Greek Automobile Club (ΕΛΠΑ) offering free roadside assistance similar to that given by A.A. mobile patrols.

Roads are extremely variable in quality.   There is a good trunk road from the Yugoslav frontier (Ithomeni) to Salonica and Athens, another to Corinth and a well-constructed coast road from Athens to Sunium.   Otherwise roads to the main towns, though usually metalled, are often narrow and sometimes in poor repair.   Roads to villages and small towns are often un-metalled. Dangers include level-crossings, often unguarded and usually involving a sharp bend in the road, mountain roads without fences, and, at night, many lorries which drive fast and use their lights inconsiderately. Road works, piles of sand, etc., are sometimes unlighted at night.   Night driving between towns, in fact, is uncomfortable.

Road signs are pictorial, as used generally throughout Europe, and easy to understand.   The A.A. Foreign Touring guide has an illustrated list of these signs.   Two important written signs are ΚΙΝΔΥΝΟΣ (**Danger**) and ΠΡΟΣΟΧΗ (**Take care**) Sign-posts showing the direction and distance of towns are clearly written in Greek and in English transliteration of the Greek pronunciation.   Thus **Athens**, for example, appears as ATHINAI and **Salonica** as THESSALONIKI.   Distances, of course, are in kilometres.

Vehicles drive on the right and overtake on the left, as in other Continental countries. Traffic lights in Athens and Salonica use the red, amber and green sequence, as in Britain, but elsewhere a simple red and green hanging light may be met with. Late at night some traffic lights are switched to emit amber flashes, which mean "proceed with caution". Pedestrian crossings in Athens are strictly controlled by lights. Policemen on point duty use clear gestures to show their meaning; you should not proceed if the policeman has his back to you, but if he has his side or front to you, you may proceed, unless he bars your way with his arm.

The use of the horn is forbidden in built-up areas, though to be recommended when overtaking in the country.

Parking is controlled, and in Athens there are certain parking places reserved for cars with foreign number-plates.

VOCABULARY

GENERAL

accident, τό δυστύχημα (tó **th**istíhima)
bicycle, τό ποδήλατο (tó po**th**ílato)
breakdown truck (*with crane*), ὁ γερανός (ό yeranós)
bus, τό λεωφορεῖο (tó leoforío)
can (*petrol*), τό μπετόνι (tó betóni)
car, τό αὐτοκίνητο (tó aftokínito)
car licence, ἡ ἄδεια κυκλοφορίας (í á**th**ia kikloforías)
caravan, τό τροχόσπιτο (tó trohóspito)
cart, τό κάρρο (tó káro)
collision, ἡ σύγκρουση (í síngkroosi)
convertible, τό ντεκαποτάμπλ (tó dekapotábl)
distilled water, τό ὑγρό μπαταρίας (tó ighró batarías)
to drive, ὁδηγῶ (o**th**ighó)
driver, ὁ ὁδηγός (ó o**th**ighós)
driving licence, ἡ ἄδεια ὁδηγήσεως (í á**th**ia o**th**iyíseos)
fine, τό πρόστιμο (tó próstimo)
garage, τό συνεργεῖο, τό γκαράζ (tó sineryío, tó garáz)
highway code, ὁ κῶδιξ ὁδικῆς κυκλοφορίας (ó kó**th**iks o**th**ikís kikloforías)
insurance, ἡ ἀσφάλεια (í asfália)
lorry, τό φορτηγό (tó fortighó)
lubrication, τό γρασάρισμα (tó ghrasárizma)
mechanic, ὁ μηχανικός (ó mihanikós)
motor-coach, τό πούλμαν (tó poólman)
motor-cycle, ἡ μοτοσυκλέτα (í motosikléta)
motorway, ὁ αὐτοκινητόδρομος (ό aftokinitó**thr**omos)
number-plate, ὁ ἀριθμός (ό arithmós)
oil, τό λάδι (tó lá**thi**)
oil (*high-pressure, for gear-boxes*), ἡ βαλβολίνη (í valvolíni)
pedestrian, ὁ πεζός (ó pezós)
petrol, ἡ βενζίνη (í venzíni)
   (*note that* πετρέλαιο—petréleo—*means* **diesel fuel**)

pump, ἡ ἀντλία (í andlía)
scooter, τό σκοῦτερ (tó skoóter)
skid, τό ντεραπάρισμα (tó derapárizma)
speed, ἡ ταχύτητα (í tahítita)
traffic, ἡ κυκλοφορία (í kikloforía)
traffic-lights, οἱ σηματοδότες (í simatothótes)
traffic policeman, ὁ τροχονόμος (ó trohonómos)
two-stroke mixture, τό μίγμα δίχρονο (tó míghma thíhrono)
vehicle, τό ὄχημα (tó óhima)

CAR

back-axle, τό πίσω ἀξόνι (tó píso aksóni)
body, ἡ καροσερί (í karoserí)
bolt, ἡ βίδα (í vítha)
bonnet, τό καπώ (tó kapó)
boot, τό πόρτ-μπαγκάζ (tó pórt-bagáz)
brake, τό φρένο (tó fréno)
brake (*hand*), τό χειρόφρενο (tó hirófreno)
brake lining, τό φερμουίτ (tó fermooít)
bumper, ὁ προφυλακτήρας (ó profilaktíras)
cap, ἡ τάπα (í tápa)
car, τό αὐτοκίνητο (tó aftokiníto)
clutch, τό ἀμπραγιάζ (tó ambrayáz)
chassis, τό σασσί (tó sasí)
differential, τό διαφορικό (tó thiaforikó)
dipstick, ὁ δείκτης (ó thíktis)
door, ἡ πόρτα (í pórta)
door-handle, τό χερούλι (tó heroóli)
exhaust, ἡ ἐξάτμηση (í eksátmisi)
funnel, τό χωνί (tó honí)
fuse, ἡ ἀσφάλεια (í asfália)
gear-box, τό κιβώτιο ταχυτήτων (tó kivótio tahitíton)
gear-lever, ὁ λεβιές (ó levyés)
glass (*window*), τό τζάμι (tó tzámi)
handle (*starting*), ἡ μανιβέλλα (í manivéla)
hood (*folding top*), ἡ κουκούλα (í kookoóla)
horn, τό κλάξον (tó klákson)
hub, τό ἀκραξόνιο (tó akraksónyo)
ignition key, τό κλειδί (tó klithí)
indicator, τά φῶτα πορείας (tá fóta porías)
inner tube, ἡ σαμπρέλλα (í sambréla)
jack, ὁ γρῖλλος (ó ghrílos)
lead (*electrical*), τό καλώδιο (tó kalóthyo)
lever, ὁ λεβιές (ó levyés)
lights (*head*), τά φανάρια (tá fanárya)
       (*side*), τά μικρά φῶτα (tá mikrá fóta)
       (*tail*), τά πίσω φῶτα (tá píso fóta)
mirror, ὁ καθρέπτης (ó kathréptis)
nut, τό παξιμάδι (tó paksimáthi)
propeller shaft, ὁ κεντρικός ἄξονας (ó kendrikós áksonas)

radiator, τό ψυγεῖο (tó psiyío)
reverse, ὄπισθεν (ópisthen)
rim, ἡ ζάντα (í zánda)
screw up, βιδώνω (vithóno)
screw, ἡ βίδα (í vítha)
screw-driver, τό κατσαβίδι (tó katsavíthi)
shock-absorber, τό ἀμορτισέρ (tó amortisér)
spanner, τό κλειδί ἀγγλικό (tó klithi anglikó)
spare parts, τά ἀνταλλακτικά (tá andalaktiká)
spare wheel, ἡ ρεζέρβα (í rezérva)
speedometer, τό κοντέρ (tó kónder)
spring (*leaf*), ἡ σοῦστα (í soósta)
     (*coil*), τό ἐλατήριο (tó elatírio)
steering-wheel, τό τιμόνι (tó timóni)
tank, τό ρεζερβουάρ (tó rezervooár)
tyre, τό λάστιχο (tó lástiho)
unscrew, ξεβιδώνω (ksevithóno)
washer, ἡ ροδέλλα (í rothéla)
wheel, ἡ ρόδα (í rótha)
windscreen, τό πάρ-μπρίζ (tó pár-bríz)
windscreen-wiper, ὁ γυαλοκαθαριστήρας (ó yalokatharistíras)
wing, τό φτερό (tó fteró)

ENGINE

accelerator, τό γκάζι (tó gázi)
battery, ἡ μπαταρία (í bataría)
big-end, ἡ κεφαλή (διωστῆρος) (í kefalí (thiostíros)
camshaft, ὁ ἐκκεντροφόρος (ó ekkendrofóros)
carburettor, τό καρμπυρατέρ (tó karbiratér)
choke, ἡ μανέτα ἀέρος (í manéta aéros)
crank-case, ὁ στροφαλοθάλαμος (ó strofalothálamos)
crankshaft, ὁ στρόφαλος, ὁ στροφαλοφόρος ἄξονας (ó strófalos, strofalofóros áksonas)
cylinder, ὁ κύλινδρος (ó kílinthros)
cylinder-block, τό μπλόκ (tó blók)
distributor, τό ντιστριμπιτέρ (tó distribitér)
dynamo, τό δυναμό (tó thinamó)
engine, ἡ μηχανή (í mihaní)
fan, τό βεντιλατέρ (tó vendilatér)
fan-belt, τό λουρί (tó loorí)
feed, ὁ τροφοδότης (ó trofothótís)
filter, τό φίλτρο (tó fíltro)
gasket, τό παρέμβασμα (tó parémvazma)
ignition, ὁ διακόπτης (o thiakóptis)
piston, τό πιστόνι (tó pistóni)
piston-rings, τά ἐλατήρια (tá elatíria)
plug, τό μπουζί (tó boozí)
pump, ἡ ἀντλία (í andlía)
spark, ὁ σπινθήρας (ó spinthíras)
starter, ἡ μίζα (í míza)

sump, τό κάρτερ (tó kárter)
timing, ὁ χρονισμός (ó hronizmós)
valve, ἡ βαλβίδα (í valvítha)

I want some petrol (oil, Θέλω βενζίνη (λάδι, νερό).
water).
thélo venzíni (láthi, neró)

Give me two (three, four) Δῶστε μου δύο (τρία, τέσσερα)
gallons. γαλόνια.
thóstemoo thío (tría, tésera) ghalónia
(*petrol is sold by the gallon in Greece*)

Fill it up. Γέμισέ το.
yémiséto

You have not given me the Τά ρέστα δέν εἶναι σωστά.
correct change.
tá résta thén íne sostá

Check the tyre pressure, Κυττάξτε τά λάστιχα παρα-
please. καλῶ.
kitákste tá lástiha, parakaló

How much (air) do you put Πόσο βάζετε;
in?
póso vázete?

Twenty-two (p.s.i.) in the Εἴκοσι δύο μπροστά καί εἴκοσι
front and twenty-four at τέσσερα πίσω.
the back.
íkosi thío brostá ké íkosi tésera píso

Can you change the oil, Μπορεῖτε ν'ἀλλάξετε τό λάδι
please? παρακαλῶ;
boríte naláksete tó láthi, parakaló

Check the oil-level in the Κυττάξτε τήν βαλβολίνη παρα-
gear-box. καλῶ.
kitákste tín valvolíni, parakaló

Put some distilled water in Βάλτε ὑγρό στήν μπαταρία
the battery, please. παρακαλῶ.
válte ighró stín bataría, parakaló

Don't overfill it. Νά μήν ξεχειλήση.
ná mín ksehilísi

Grease it, please.	Γρασάρισμα παρακαλῶ.
	ghrasárizma, parakaló
Oil this, please.	Λαδῶστε αὐτό παρακαλῶ.
	lathóste aftó, parakaló
Wash the car, please.	Πλύνετε τό αὐτοκίνητο παρακαλῶ.
	plínete tó aftokínito, parakaló
Please wipe this.	Καθαρῖστε ἐδῶ παρακαλῶ.
	katharíste ethó, parakaló
Can I garage the car for the night (a week)?	Μπορῶ ν'ἀφήσω τό αὐτοκίνητο στό γκαράζ γιά μιά νύχτα (μιά βδομάδα);
	boró nafíso tó aftokínito stó garáz yá miá níhta (miá vthomáthá)?
What time does the garage close?	Τί ὥρα κλείνει τό γκαράζ;
	tí óra klíni tó garáz?
Is the garage open all night?	Διανυκτερεύει τό γκαράζ;
	thianikterévi tó garáz?
I want to leave early tomorrow.	Θέλω νά ξεκινήσω νωρίς αὔριο.
	thélo ná ksekiníso norís ávrio
Where is the owner of the garage?	Ποῦ εἶναι τό ἀφεντικό τοῦ γκαράζ;
	poó íne tó afendikó toó garáz?
Do you do repairs?	Κάνετε ἐπισκευές;
	kánete episkevés?
Can you repair . . .?	Μπορεῖτε νά διορθώσετε . . .;
	boríte ná thiorthósete . . .?
This does not work.	Αὐτό δέν δουλεύει.
	aftó thén thoolévi
My car has stopped.	Τό αὐτοκίνητό μου σταμάτησε.
	tó aftokínitómoo stamátise
I've had a puncture.	Ἔχω λάστιχο.
	ého lástiho
This tyre is punctured.	Αὐτό τό λάστιχο ἔχει τρυπήσει.
	aftó tó lástiho éhi tripísi
My tyre has burst.	Τό λάστιχό μου ἔσκασε.
	tó lástihómoo éskase

My car (motor-cycle) has stopped on the road two kilometres away. Τό αὐτοκίνητό μου (ἡ μοτο-συκλέττα) ἔμεινε στό δρόμο, δυό χιλιόμετρα μακρυά.

to aftokínitómoo (i motosiklétamoo) émine stó thrómo, thió hiliómetra makryá

Can you send someone? Μπορεῖτε νά στείλετε κάποιον;

boríte ná stílete kápyon?

What's the matter with it? Τί ἔχει;

tí éhi?

I don't know. Δέν ξέρω.

thén kséro

I've run out of petrol. Ἔμεινα ἀπό βενζίνη.

émina apó venzíni

It has gone off the road. Βγῆκε ἀπ'τό δρόμο.

vyíke ap tó thrómo

It is in the ditch. Ἔπεσε σέ χαντάκι.

épese sé handáki

It hit a tree (rock). Ἔπεσε σέ δέντρο (βράχο).

épese sé théndro (vráho)

There has been a collision. Ἔγινε σύγκρουση.

éyine síngkroosi

The . . . is broken. Ἔσπασε τό . . .

éspase tó . . .

There is a dent here. Ἔχει ἕνα χτύπημα ἐδῶ.

éhi éna htípima ethó

Can you beat it out? Μπορεῖτε νά τό στρώσετε;

boríte ná tó strósete?

Can you tow the car? Μπορεῖτε νά ρυμουλκήσετε τό αὐτοκίνητο;

boríte ná rimoolkísete tó aftokínito?

This must be replaced. Αὐτό θέλει ἀντικατάσταση.

aftó théli andikatástasi

This needs straightening. Αὐτό πρέπει νά ἰσιώνη.

aftó prépi ná isióni

The car needs to be over-hauled. Τό αὐτοκίνητο χρειάζεται γενικό ἔλεγχο.

tó aftokínito hriázete yenikó élengho

Can you do it at once? Μπορεῖτε νά τό κάνετε ἀμέσως;

boríte ná tó kánete amésos?

How long will it take? Πόση ὥρα θά κάνει;

pósi óra thá káni?

I am in a great hurry. I have a ship to catch. Βιάζομαι πολύ. Πρέπει νά προλάβω τό πλοῖο.

viázome polí. prépi ná prolávo tó plío

The engine is misfiring. Ἡ λειτουργία τοῦ κινητῆρος εἶναι διακοπτομένη.

i litooryía toó kinitíros íne thiakoptoméni

The plug is dirty. Τό μπουζί θέλει καθάρισμα.

tó boozí théli kathárizma

It is knocking (squeak-ing). Χτυπάει (τρίζει).

htipái (trízi)

It won't open (shut, lock). Δέν ἀνοίγει (κλείνει, κλειδώνει).

thén aníyi (klíni, klithóni)

The engine is overheating. Ἡ μηχανή ζεσταίνεται πολύ.

i mihaní zesténete polí

The . . . doesn't work very well. Τό . . . δέν δουλεύει καλά.

tó . . . thén thoolévi kalá

There is a leak in the . . . Τό . . . τρέχει.

tó . . . tréhi

The carburettor is choked. Βούλωσε τό καρμπιρατέρ.

voólose tó karbiratér

Clean out the carburettor, please. Καθαρίστε τό καρμπιρατέρ, παρακαλῶ.

katharíste tó karbiratér, parakaló

The battery is not charging. Ἡ μπαταρία δέν φορτώνει.

i bataría thén fortóni

May I borrow . . . ? Μπορεῖτε νά μοῦ δανείσετε . . . ;

boríte ná moó thanísete . . . ?

You will need . . . Θά χρειαστῆτε . . .

thá hriastíte . . .

Can you drive? Ξέρετε νά ὁδηγῆτε
ksérete ná othiyíte?

He drives (does not drive) well. Ὁδηγεῖ (δέν ὁδηγεῖ) καλά.
othiyí (thén othiyí) kalá

The car is skidding. Τό αὐτοκίνητο γλυστράει.
tó aftokínito ghlistrái

Start! Stop! Ξεκίνα! Σταμάτα!
ksekína! stamáta!

Go into second (third, fourth, reverse) gear. Βάλε δεύτερη, (τρίτη, τετάρτη, ὄπισθεν) ταχύτητα.
vále théfteri (tríti, tetárti, ópisthen) tahítita

Screw it up. Βίδωσέ το.
víthoséto

Tighter. Not so tight. Πιό σφιχτά. Ὄχι τόσο σφιχτά.
pyó sfihtá. óhi tóso sfihtá

Careful! Σιγά!
sighá!

Put it here. Βάλτο ἐδῶ.
válto ethó

Take that off. Βγάλε αὐτό.
vghále aftó

I have lost all my documents. Ἔχασα ὅλα τά χαρτιά μου.
éhasa óla tá hartyámoo

I want to hire a car (motorcycle, scooter, bicycle) Θέλω νά νοικιάσω ἕνα αὐτοκίνητο (μοτοσυκλέττα, σκοῦτερ, ποδήλατο).
thélo ná nikyáso éna aftokínito (motosikléta, skoóter, pothílato)

For the day only. Γιά μιά μέρα μόνο.
yá miá méra móno

Where do you want to go? Πού θέλετε νά πᾶτε;
poó thélete ná páte?

How long do you want it? Γιά πόσο τό θέλετε;
yá póso tó thélete?

Have you a licence?	Ἔχετε ἄδεια;
	éhete áthia?
Yes. This is an International Driving Licence.	Ναί. Αὐτή εἶναι Διεθνής Ἄδεια.
	né. aftí íne thiethnís áthia
How much is it for the day (hour, week)?	Πόσο κάνει τήν ἡμέρα (τήν ὥρα, τήν ἑβδομάδα);
	póso káni tín iméra (tín óra, tín evthomátha)?
Two drachmas a kilometre. Petrol included.	Δυό δραχμές τό χιλιόμετρο. Μέ τή βενζίνη.
	thió thrahmés tó hiliómetro. mé tín venzíni
Is there a minimum charge?	Ὑπάρχει μίνιμουμ χρέωσις;
	ipárhi mínimoom hréosis?
Is it insured? Show me the contract.	Εἶναι ἀσφαλισμένο; Δεῖξε μου τό συμβόλαιο.
	íne asfalizméno? thíksemoo tó simvóleo
Show me how the gears work. The lights.	Δεῖξε μου τίς ταχύτητες. Τά φῶτα.
	thíksemoo tís tahítites. tá fóta
I want a car with driver.	Θέλω ἕνα αὐτοκίνητο μέ ὁδηγό.
	thélo éna aftokínito mé othighó
Do you know the road to . . .?	Ξέρετε τό δρόμο γιά . . .;
	ksérete tó thrómo yá . . .?
We want to tour the district.	Θέλωμε νά γυρίσουμε τήν περιοχή.
	thélome ná yirísoome tín periohí
Where can we lunch?	Πού μποροῦμε νά φᾶμε;
	poó boroóme ná fáme?
Is there a good beach near here?	Ὑπάρχει καμιά καλή θάλασσα ἐδῶ κοντά;
	ipárhi kamyá kalí thálasa ethó kondá?
Do not go so fast.	Μήν τρέχεις τόσο.
	mí tréhis tóso
Wait for us here (over there)	Περίμενέ μας ἐδῶ (ἐκεῖ).
	perímenémas ethó (ekí)
Stop at the corner.	Σταμάτησε στή γωνία.
	stamátise stí ghonía

We are going to see . . .	Θά πᾶμε νά δοῦμε τό . . .
	thá páme ná thoóme tó . . .
We are going to lunch here.	Θά φᾶμε ἐδῶ.
	thá fáme ethó
Pick us up at the station at four-thirty.	Ἔλα νά μᾶς πάρης στό σταθμό στίς τέσσερις καί μισή.
	éla ná más páris stó stathmó stís téseris ké misí
We must be back by . . .	Πρέπει νά ἥμαστε πίσω μέχρι . . .
	prépi ná ímaste píso méhri . . .
What is the matter? Why have you stopped?	Τί τρέχει; Γιατί σταμάτησες;
	tí tréhi? yatí stamátises?

TRAVEL

VOCABULARY

airport, τό ἀεροδρόμιο (tó aero**th**rómio)
arrival, ἡ ἄφιξις (i áfiksis)
bag, ἡ σακκούλα (i sakoóla)
boat, τό πλοῖο (tó plío)
camera, ἡ φωτογραφική μηχανή (i fotoghrafikí mihaní)
cardboard box, τό χαρτοκιβώτιο (tó hartokivótio)
cigar, τό ποῦρο (tó poóro)
cigarette, τό τσιγάρο (tó tsigháro)
Customs, τό Τελωνεῖο (tó telonío)
customs officer, ὁ Τελώνης (o telónis)
declare, to, δηλώνω (thilóno)
departure, ἡ ἀναχώρησις (i anahórisis)
gangway, ἡ σκάλα (i skála)
handbag, ἡ τσάντα (i tsánda)
item, τό κομμάτι (tó komáti)
key, τό κλειδί (tó kli**th**í)
label, ἡ ἐτικέττα (i etikéta)
luggage, οἱ ἀποσκευές (i aposkevés)
number, ὁ ἀριθμός, τό νούμερο (o arithmós, tó noómero)
overcoat, τό παλτό (tó paltó)
parcel, τό δέμα (tó **th**éma)
passport, τό διαβατήριο (tó **th**iavatírio)
port, τό λιμάνι (tó limáni)
porter, ὁ ἀχθοφόρος (o ah**th**ofóros)
raincoat, τό ἀδιάβροχο (tó a**th**iávroho)
station, ὁ σταθμός (o stathmós)
suitcase, ἡ βαλίτσα (i valítsa)

tobacco, ὁ καπνός (o kapnós)
train, τό τραῖνο (tó tréno)
trunk, τό μπαοῦλο (tó baoólo)
umbrella, ἡ ὀμπρέλλα (i ombréla)

Your passport, please.   Τό διαβατήριό σας, παρακαλῶ.
to thiavatíriósas, parakaló

My wife is on my passport.   Ἡ γυναίκα μου εἶναι στό δικό
μου διαβατήριο.
i yinékamoo íne stó thikómoo thiavatírio

The child (children) is on   Τό παιδί (τά παιδιά) εἶναι
this passport.   σ'αὐτό τό διαβατήριο.
tó pethí (tá pethyá) íne saftó tó thiavatírio

How much money have you?   Πόσα χρήματα ἔχετε;
pósa hrímata éhete?

£100 in Traveller's Cheques   Ἑκατό λίρες σέ ταξιδιωτικά
and 2,000 drachmas.   τσέκ καί δύο χιλιάδες δραχμές.
ekató líres sé taksithiotiká tsék ké thío hiliáthes thrahmés

Porter, this way.   Ἀχθοφόρε, ἀπ'ἐδῶ.
ahthofóre, apothó

Here is my luggage.   Νά οἱ ἀποσκευές μου.
ná í aposkevésmoo

Your number?   Ὁ ἀριθμός σας;
o arithmóssas?

Just these?   Αὐτά μόνο;
aftá móno?

Have you any more?   Ἔχετε ἄλλα;
éhete álla?

I only have a suitcase and a   Ἔχω μόνο μιά βαλίτσα καί ἕνα
bag.   σάκκο.
ého móno miá valítsa ké éna sákko

I shall take this myself.   Αὐτό θά τό πάρω μόνος μου.
aftó thá tó páro mónosmoo

Do not take that.   Μήν πάρῃς αὐτό.
mín páris aftó

| This is not mine. | Αὐτό δέν εἶναι δικό μου. |
| | aftó thén íne thikómoo |

| Be very careful with that. | Ἐκεῖνο, μέ πολύ προσοχή. |
| | ekíno mé polí prosohí |

| Look out! The lock (handle) is broken. | Πρόσεχε! Ἡ κλειδαριά (τό χερούλι) ἔσπασε. |
| | prósehe! i klithariá (to heroóli) éspase |

| There is another bag there. | Ἐδῶ εἶναι κι'ἄλλη βαλίτσα. |
| | ethó íne kyáli valítsa |

| Don't leave this. Don't forget that. | Μήν τ'ἀφήνεις αὐτό. Μήν ξεχάσεις ἐκεῖνο. |
| | mín tafínis aftó. min ksehásis ekíno |

| Have you anything to declare? | Ἔχετε νά δηλώσετε τίποτα; |
| | éhete ná thilósete típota? |

| Have you filled in your declaration? | Συμπληρώσατε τή δήλωσή σας; |
| | simblirósate tí thilosísas? |

| Nothing. | Τίποτα. |
| | típota |

| Cigarettes, scent? | Τσιγάρα, ἀρώματα; |
| | tsighára, arómata? |

| What's in there? | Τί ἔχετε ἐδῶ; |
| | tí éhete ethó? |

| Nothing. Only clothes. | Τίποτα. Ροῦχα μόνο. |
| | típota. roóha móno |

| Open this suitcase. | Ἄνοιξε αὐτή τή βαλίτσα. |
| | ánikse aftí tí valítsa |

| I have lost my keys. | Ἔχασα τά κλειδιά μου. |
| | éhasa tá klithyámoo |

| I cannot open it. | Δέν μπορῶ νά τήν ἀνοίξω. |
| | thén boró ná tín aníkso |

| All that is for my personal use. | Εἶναι ὅλα προσωπικῆς χρήσεως. |
| | íne óla prosopikís hríseos |

| Have you any other luggage? | Ἔχετε ἄλλες ἀποσκευές; |
| | éhete áles aposkevés? |

Have you anything of value? Ἔχετε τίποτα ἀξίας;
éhete típota aksías?

I have a camera (cine-camera, typewriter, radio). Ἔχω φωτογραφική μηχανή (κινηματογραφική μηχανή, γραφομηχανή, ραδιόφωνο).
ého fotoghrafikí mihaní (kinimatoghrafikí mihaní, ghrafomihaní, rathiófono)

This is all I have. Αὐτά εἶναι ὅλα πού ἔχω.
aftá íne óla poóého

My luggage has been examined. Οἱ ἀποσκευές μου ἐλέγχθηκαν.
i aposkevésmoo elénghthikan

This is already marked. Αὐτό ἔχει σημειωθεῖ.
aftó éhi simiothí

You have not marked that. Δέν τό σημειώσατε αὐτό.
thén tó simiósate aftó

Help me to close this case. Βοηθῆστε με νά κλείσω αὐτή τή βαλίτσα.
voithísteme ná klíso aftí tí valítsa

I did not know that I had to pay. Δέν ἤξερα ὅτι ἔπρεπε νά πλήρώσω.
thén íksera óti éprepe ná plíroso

I cannot find my porter. Δέν βρίσκω τόν ἀχθοφόρο.
thén vrísko tón ahthofóro

What is his number? Ποιό εἶναι τό νούμερό του; (ὁ ἀριθμός του)
pyó íne tó noómerótoo? (ó arithmóstoo?)

I have forgotten. Τὄχω ξεχάσει.
tóho ksehási

Have you seen porter No....? Μήπως εἴδατε τόν ἀχθοφόρο No...;
mípos íthate tón ahthofóro noómero...?

How much do I owe you? Πόσο σᾶς χρωστάω;
póso sás hrostáo?

Whatever you like. Ὅτι θέλ ꞏτε.
óti thélete

Find me a taxi. Βρέστε μου ἕνα ταξί.
vréstemoo éna taksí

TRAINS

The cheapest way of getting to Greece from England is by train via Ostend. The journey takes three days and is not particularly comfortable.

In Greece itself most of the larger towns are served by the railway, though the trains are not very fast. Information and tickets may be had at any travel-agent's; intending passengers should reserve their seats in advance.

VOCABULARY

berth (*couchette*), ἡ κουκέτα (i kookéta); (*at the time of writing couchettes had not been seen in Greece*)

blanket, ἡ κουβέρτα (i koovérta)

booking-office, τό γκισέ (tó gishé)

bookstall, τό περίπτερο (tó períptero)

bridge, ἡ γέφυρα (í yéfira)

carriage, τό βαγόνι (tó vaghóni)

cloakroom (*left luggage*), ἡ αἴθουσα ἀποσκευῶν (í éthoosa aposkevón)

compartment, τό διαμέρισμα (tó **thi**amérizma)

communication cord, τό σῆμα κινδύνου (tó síma kinthínoo)

corridor, ὁ διάδρομος (o **thi**áthromos)

diesel rail-car, τό ὠτομοτρίς (tó otomotrís)

dining-car, τό ρεστωράν. τό ἐστιατόριο (tó restorán, tó estiatório)

door, ἡ πόρτα (í pórta)

engine, ἡ μηχανή (í mihaní)

enquiry, πληροφορίαι (pliroforíe)

entrance, ἡ εἴσοδος (í ísothos)

exit, ἡ ἔξοδος (í éksothos)

express, ἡ ταχεῖα (í tahía)

footboard, τό σκαλοπάτι (tó skalopáti)

gate, ἡ εἴσοδος (í ísothos)

guard, ὁ συνοδός (ó sinothós)

journey, τό ταξίδι (tó taksíthi)

level-crossing, ἡ ἰσόπεδος διάβασις (í isópe**th**os **thi**ávasis)

luggage-van, τό βαγόνι ἀποσκευῶν (tó vaghóni aposkevón)

passenger, ὁ ἐπιβάτης (ó epivátis)

pillow, τό μαξιλάρι (tó maksilári)

platform, ἡ πλατφόρμα (í platfórma)

rack, τό δίχτυ (tó **th**íhti)

rails, ἡ ράγια (í ráya)

railway, ὁ σιδηρόδρομος (o sithiróthromos)

refreshment room, τό ἀναψυκτήριον (tó anapsiktírion)

seat, ἡ θέσις (í thésis)

seat reservation, κλείσιμο θέσης (klísimo thésis)

sleeping car, τό βαγκόν-λί (tó vagón-lí)

smoking compartment, τό διαμέρισμα καπνιστῶν (tó **thi**amérizma kapnistón)

station, ὁ σταθμός (ó stathmós)

station-master, ὁ σταθμάρχης (ó stathmárhis)
subway, ἡ ὑπόγεια διάβασις (í ipóyia thiávasis)
ticket, εἰσιτίριον (isitírion)
return ticket, εἰσιτίριον μετ'ἐπιστροφῆς (isitírion metepistrofís)
ticket collector, ὁ ἐλεγκτής (ó elengktís)
time-table, τό δρομολόγιον (tó thromolóyion)
track, οἱ γραμμές (í ghramés)
train, τό τραῖνο (tó tréno)
toilet, ἡ τουαλέττα (í tooaléta)
tunnel, τό τοῦνελ (tó toónel)
waiting-room, ἡ αἴθουσα ἀναμονῆς (í éthoosa anamonís)
window, τό παράθυρο (tó paráthiro)

PUBLIC NOTICES

ΑΦΙΞΙΣ (áfiksis) = **Arrival**
ΑΝΑΧΩΡΗΣΙΣ (anahórisis) = **Departure**
ΕΙΣΟΔΟΣ (ísothos) = **Entrance**
ΕΞΟΔΟΣ (éksothos) = **Exit**
ΑΝΔΡΩΝ (anthrón) = **Gentlemen**
ΓΥΝΑΙΚΩΝ (yinekón) = **Ladies**
ΑΠΑΓΟΡΕΥΕΤΑΙ Η ΕΙΣΟΔΟΣ (apaghorévete i ísothos) = **No Entrance**
ΤΗΛΕΦΩΝΟ (tiléfono) = **Telephone**
ΕΙΣΙΤΗΡΙΑ (isitíria) = **Tickets**

What time does the train for . . . leave? Τί ὥρα φεύγει τό τραῖνο γιά . . .;
tí óra févyi tó tréno yá . . .?

What time does it arrive? Τί ὥρα φθάνει;
tí óra fth'áni?

Does this go to . . .? Πηγαίνει αὐτό στό . . .;
piyéni aftó stó . . .?

Please help me up (down). Παρακαλῶ βοηθῆστε με ν'ἀνεβῶ (να κατεβῶ).
parakaló voithísteme nanevó (na katevó)

Please pass me that case. Παρακαλῶ μοῦ δίνετε ἐκείνη τή βαλίτσα;
parakaló moó thínete ekíni tí valítsa?

I have two first-class seats (second-class) reserved. Ἔχω κλείσει δύο θέσεις πρώτης (δευτέρας).
ého klísi thío thésis prótis (theftéras)

Find me a smoking (non-smoking) compartment. Βρῆτε μου διαμέρισμα (μή) καπνιστῶν.
vrítemoo thiamérizma (mí) kapnistón

Find me a corner seat.	Δῶστε μου μία θέση στό παρά-θυρο.
	thóstemoo mía thési stó paráthiro

I want a seat by the window.	Θέλω μιά θέση κοντά στό παράθυρο.
	thélo mía thési kondá stó paráthiro

Facing the engine. Back to the engine.	Μέ κατεύθυνση τή μηχανή. ᾽Αντίθετα στή μηχανή.
	mé katéfthinsi tí mihaní. andítheta stí mihaní

Put the cases on the rack.	Βᾶλτε τίς βαλίτσες στό δίχτυ.
	válte tís valítses stó thíhti

This seat is reserved.	Αὐτή ἡ θέση εἶναι πιασμένη.
	aftí í thési íne piazméni

The numbers are the same.	Οἱ ἀριθμοί εἶναι ἴδιοι.
	i arithmí íne íthyi

Where is the ticket collector?	Ποῦ εἶναι ὁ ἐλεγκτής;
	poó íne ó elengktís?

Find me another seat.	Βρῆτε μου μιά ἄλλη θέση.
	vrítemoo miá áli thési

Near the dining-car.	Κοντά στό ἐστιατόριο.
	kondá stó estiatório

Are there any first-class seats?	῾Υπάρχουν εἰσιτήρια πρώτης θέσης;
	ipárhoon isitíria prótis thésis?

I shall pay the excess.	Θά πληρώσω τή διαφορά.
	thá pliróso tí thiaforá

Someone has taken my seat.	Κάποιος πῆρε τή θέση μου.
	kápyos píre tí thésimoo

Excuse me, sir, that seat is mine.	Μέ συγχωρεῖτε, κύριε, αὐτή ἡ θέση εἶναι δική μου.
	mé singhoríte, kírie, aftí i thési íne thikímoo

I cannot find my ticket.	Δέν βρίσκω τό εἰσιτήριό μου.
	thén vrísko tó isitíriómoo

Wait while I look for it.	Περιμένετε νά ψάξω.
	periménete ná psákso

I have left my ticket in the compartment.
Ἄφησα τό εἰσιτήριό μου στήν θέση μου.
áfisa tó isitíriómoo stín thésimoo

I shall go and look for it.
Θά πάω νά ψάξω.
thá páo ná psákso

I have left my bag (gloves, book, glasses) in the dining-car.
Ξέχασα τή τσάντα μου (γάντια, βιβλίο, γυαλιά) στό ἑστιατόριο.
kséhasa ti tsándamoo (tá ghándia, tó vivlío, tá yalyá) stó estiatório

Have you found it?
Τό βρήκατε;
to vríkate?

What is the matter?
Τί συμβαίνει;
tí simvéni?

When do we get to . . .?
Πότε φθάνουμε στό . . .;
póte fthánoome stó . . .?

Tickets, please!
Εἰσιτήρια, παρακαλῶ!
isitíria, parakaló

This seat is unoccupied (taken).
Αὐτή ἡ θέση εἶναι ἄδεια (πιασμένη).
aftí í thési íne áthia (piazméni)

May I open the window?
Μπορῶ ν'ἀνοίξω τό παράθυρο;
boró naníkso tó paráthiro?

Can you help me to open this window, please?
Μέ βοηθᾶτε ν'ἀνοίξουμε αὐτό τό παράθυρο, παρακαλῶ;
mé voitháte naníksoome aftó tó paráthiro, parakaló?

Where is the toilet?
Πού εἶναι ἡ τουαλέττα;
poó íne i tooaléta?

Are there any vacant berths in the sleeper?
Ὑπάρχουν κρεβάτια ἐλεύθερα στό βαγκόν—λί;
ipárhoon krevátia eléfthera stó vagón-lí?

Where is the dining-car?
Πού εἶναι τό ἑστιατόριο;
poó íne tó estiatório?

At the front (back) of the train.
Στό μπροστινό μέρος (πίσω) τοῦ τραίνου.
stó brostinó (píso) méros toó trénoo

Will you take lunch (dinner), sir?	Θά γευματίσετε (δειπνείσετε) Κύριε; thá yevmatísete (thipnísete) kírie?
What time do you serve lunch, (dinner)?	Τί ὥρα σερβίρετε γεῦμα (δεῖπνο); tí óra servírete yévma (thípno)?
I want to leave my luggage here.	Θέλω ν'ἀφήσω τίς βαλίτσες μου ἐδῶ. thélo nafíso tís valítsesmoo ethó
I want to put this in the left-luggage office.	Θέλω ν'ἀφήσω αὐτό στήν αἴθουσα ἀποσκευῶν. thélo nafíso aftó stín éthoosa aposkevón
Do I pay now?	Θά πληρώσω τώρα; thá pliróso tóra?
I shall take them out this evening.	Θά τίς πάρω ἀπόψε. thá tís páro apópse
I am leaving by the nine o'clock train.	Φεύγω μέ τό τραῖνο τῶν ἐννέα. févgho mé tó tréno tón enéa
I want to take out these three things.	Θέλω νά βγάλω αὐτά τά τρία κομμάτια. thélo ná vghálo aftá tá tría komátia
How much do I owe you?	Πόσο σᾶς χρωστάω; póso sás hrostáo?
This one is not mine.	Αὐτή δέν εἶναι δική μου. aftí thén íne thikímoo
Where is the lost property office?	Πού βρίσκεται τό γραφεῖο ἀπωλεσθέντων; poó vrískete tó ghrafío apolesthéndon?
I am coming with you.	Θάρθῶ μαζί σας. thárthó mazísas
I have left something in the train.	Ξέχασα κάτι στό τραῖνο. kséhasa káti stó tréno

What did you leave? Where did you leave it?
Τί ξεχάσατε; Πού τό ξεχάσατε;
tí ksehásate? poó tó ksehásate?

A suitcase. In the rack above seat No. ... in carriage No. ...
Μία βαλίτσα. Στό δίχτυ πάνω ἀπό τό κάθισμα No. ... στό βαγόνι No. ...
mía valítsa. stó thíhti páno apó tó káthizma ... stó vagóni ..

Can it be sent to me?
Μπορεῖτε νά μοῦ τή στείλετε;
boríte ná moó tí stílete?

How much shall I have to pay?
Πόσο θά κοστίση;
póso thá kostísi?

Where do I find the registered luggage?
Πού θά βρῶ τίς συστημένες ἀποσκευές;
poó thá vró tís sistiménes aposkevés?

I have a registered trunk.
Ἔχω ἕνα μπαούλο συστημένο.
ého éna baoólo sistiméno

Can you come with me to get it out?
Ἔρχεστε μαζί μου νά τό πάρουμε;
érheste mazímoo ná tó pároome?

Here is my luggage ticket.
Νά ἡ ἀπόδειξις τῶν ἀποσκευῶν μου.
ná i apóthiksis tón aposkevónmoo

I have lost my luggage ticket.
Ἔχασα τήν ἀπόδειξη τῶν ἀποσκευῶν μου.
éhasa tín apóthiksi tón aposkevónmoo

I want to register this trunk for ...
Θέλω νά στείλω συστημένο αὐτό τό μπαούλο στήν ...
thélo ná stílo sistiméno aftó tó baoólo stín ...

I want to send it in advance.
Θέλω νά τό στείλω χωριστά.
thélo ná tó stílo horistá

I am travelling first (second).
Ταξιδεύω πρώτη (δευτέρα).
taksithévo próti (theftéra)

Here is my ticket.
Νά τό εἰσιτήριό μου.
ná tó isitíriómoo

Please give me the receipt. Δῶστε μου παρακαλῶ τήν
ἀπόδειξη.
thóstemoo parakaló tín apóthiksi

Take this luggage and find Πάρτε αὐτές τίς ἀποσκευές καί
me a taxi. βρῆτε μου ἕνα ταξί.
párte aftés tís aposkevés ké vrítemoo éna taksí

To the . . . Hotel. Στό Ξενοδοχεῖο . . .
stó ksenothohío . . .

I am in a hurry. Βιάζομαι.
viázome

To the Larissa (Peloponnese) Στό Σταθμό Λαρίσης (Πελο-
Station. πονήσου).
stó stathmó Larísis (Peloponísoo)

*From Athens, trains for mainland Greece, including Salonica and the Yugoslav
and Turkish frontiers, start from Larissa Station, while those for the
Peloponnese start from another station two hundred yards or so down the line.*

I have a train to catch. Πρέπει νά προφτάσω τό τραῖνο.
prépi ná prostáso tó tréno

What time is the first (last) Τί ὥρα φεύγει γιά . . . τό πρῶτο
train for . . . ? (τελευταῖο) τραῖνο;
tí óra févyi yá . . . tó próto (teleftéo) tréno?

Where is the booking-office? Ποῦ εἶναι τό γκισέ;
poó íne tó gishé?

Two first-class return Παρακαλῶ, δύο εἰσιτήρια
tickets for . . ., please. πρώτης θέσης γιά . . .
parakaló, thío isitíria prótis thésis yá . . .

One second-class single Ἕνα εἰσιτήριο ἄνευ ἐπιστροφῆς
for . . . γιά . . .
éna isitírio anéf epistrofís yá . . .

How much is that? Πόσο κάνει;
póso káni?

For how long is this ticket Γιά πόσο καιρό ἰσχύει αὐτό τό
valid? εἰσιτήριο;
yá póso keró iskhí aftó tó isitírio?

This ticket is no longer valid. Αὐτό τό εἰσιτήριο δέν ἰσχύει
πλέον.
aftó tó isitírio thén iskhí pléon

When does it leave? Πότε φεύγει;
póte févyi?

Is there a through train (carriage) for . . . ? Ὑπάρχει τραῖνο (βαγόνι) κατευθεῖαν γιά . . .;
ipárhi tréno (vaghóni) katefthían yá . . . ?

Must I change for . . . ? Πρέπει ν'ἀλλάξω γιά . . .;
prépi nalákso yá . . . ?

Where do I change for . . . ? Πού ν'ἀλλάξω γιά . . .;
poó nalákso yá . . . ?

Must I change here for . . . ? Πρέπει ν'ἀλλάξω ἐδῶ γιά . . .;
prépi nalákso ethó yá . . . ?

Where must I get out? Ποῦ πρέπει νά βγῶ . . .;
poó prépi ná vghó?

Is this the right train (carriage) for . . . Εἶναι αὐτό τό τραῖνο (βαγόνι) γιά τή . . .
íne aftó tó tréno (vaghóni) yá . . . ?

How long does the train stop here? Πόσο μένει τό τραῖνο ἐδῶ;
póso méni tó tréno ethó?

Does this train stop at . . . ? Σταματάει αὐτό τό τραῖνο στό . . .;
stamatái aftó tó tréno stó . . . ?

It stops at all stations. Σταματάει σέ ὅλους τούς σταθμούς.
stamatái sé óloos toós stathmoós

Has the train for . . . gone? Τό τραῖνο γιά τό . . . ἔφυγε;
tó tréno yá tó . . . éfiye?

Have I missed the train for . . . ? Ἔχασα τό τραῖνο γιά . . .;
éhasa tó tréno yá . . . ?

How long shall I have to wait? Πόσο θά περιμένω;
póso thá periméno?

Is there another train today? Ὑπάρχει ἄλλο τραῖνο γιά σήμερα;
ipárhi álo tréno yá símera?

I have got into the wrong train. Δέν μπῆκα στό σωστό τραῖνο.

thén bíka stó sostó tréno

What should I do? Τί πρέπει νά κάνω;

tí prépi ná káno?

Is there an hotel where I can stay the night? Ὑπάρχει κανένα ξενοδοχεῖο γιά νά μείνω τή νύχτα;

ipárhi kanéna ksenothohío yá ná míno tí níhta?

The last train has gone. Τό τελευταῖο τραῖνο ἔφυγε

tó telestéo tréno éfiye

PLANE

Athens is about three hours from London by direct jet flight, and somewhat longer if a stop is made at Rome. Greece is served by airlines from all the major European and Middle Eastern cities; a line which may prove useful to the British tourist is that between Brindisi in Italy, Corfu and Athens. There is besides a particularly comprehensive internal network operated by Olympic Airways, serving most of the larger towns and islands; since mountain and sea make surface travel in Greece rather slow, it is often well worth while flying from place to place, especially if one has a lot to see in a short time. Information and tickets may be had at all travel agents'.

Air hostesses on Greek aircraft all speak English, as do airport staff and booking clerks, so there should be no language difficulties.

VOCABULARY

air hostess, ἡ ἀεροσυνοδός (í aerosinothós)
airline, ἡ ἀεροπορική γραμμή (í aeroporikí ghramí)
airport, τό ἀεροδρόμιο (tó aerothrómio)
aeroplane, τό ἀεροπλάνο (tó aeropláno)
cloud, τό σύννεφο (tó sínefo)
control tower, ὁ πύργος ἐλέγχου (ó pírghos elénghoo)
cotton-wool, τό βαμβάκι (tó vamváki)
crew, τό πλήρωμα (tó plíroma)
fog, ἡ ὁμίχλη (í omíhli)
jet aircraft, τό ἀεριωθούμενο (tó aeriothoómeno)
to land, προσγειώνομαι (prozyíonome)
landing, προσγείωσις (prozyíosis)
paper bag, ἡ χαρτοσακκούλα (í hartosakoóla)
passenger, ὁ ἐπιβάτης (ó epivátis)
pilot, ὁ πιλότος (ó pilótos)
propeller, ὁ ἕλικας (ó élikas)
route, ἡ διαδρομή (í thiathromí)
runway, ὁ διάδρομος (ó thiáthromos)

seat, τό κάθισμα (τό káthizma)
seat-belt, ή ζώνη ἀσφαλείας (í zóni asfalías)
to take off, ἀπογειώνομαι (apoyiónome)
take-off, ή ἀπογείωσις (i apoyíosis)
tray, ὁ δίσκος (o thískos)
window, τό παράθυρο (τό paráthiro)
wing, τό φτερό (tó fteró)

The plane is late.

Τό ἀεροπλάνο ἄργησε.

to aeropláno áryise

The plane is landing (taking off).

Τό ἀεροπλάνο προσγειώνεται (ἀπογειώνεται).

to aeropláno prozyiónete (apoyiónete)

I want to reserve a seat on the plane leaving tomorrow for ...

Θέλω νά κλείσω μιά θέση στό ἀεροπλάνο πού φεύγει αὔριο γιά ...

thélo ná klíso miá thési stó aeropláno poó févyi ávrio yá ...

Is there a plane for ... today?

Ὑπάρχει ἀεροπλάνο γιά ... σήμερα;

ipárhi aeropláno yá ... símera?

What time does it leave?

Τί ὥρα φεύγει;

tí óra févyi?

When does it arrive at ...?

Πότε φθάνει στό ...;

póte stháni stó ...?

Does it land anywhere en route?

Προσγειώνεται καθόλου κατά τήν διαδρομή;

prozyiónete kathóloo katá tín thiathromí?

Bring me some cotton-wool, please.

Μοῦ δίνετε λίγο βαμβάκι, παρακαλῶ.

moó thínete lígho vamváki, parakaló

I do not feel well.

Δέν αἰσθάνομαι καλά.

thén esthánome kalá

Are you air-sick?

Ζαλίζεσθε;

zalízesthe?

Bring me some coffee (brandy, water) please.

Φέρτε μου λίγο καφέ (μπράντυ, νερό) παρακαλῶ.

fértemoo lígho kafé (brándy, neró) parakaló

What is that town (island, mountain)? Ποιά εἶναι αὐτή ἡ πόλις (αὐτό τό νησί, βουνό);

pyá íne aftí í pólis (aftó tó nisí, voonó)?

We shall land at ... in five minutes. Θά προσγειωθοῦμε σέ πέντε λεπτά εἰς. ...

thá prozyiothoóme sé pénde leptá ís ...

Put out your cigarettes and fasten your seat-belts, please. Σβῦστε τά τσιγάρα σας καί δέσατε τίς ζῶνες ἀσφαλείας, παρακαλῶ.

zvíste tá tsighárasas ké théste tís zónes asfalías, parakaló

I cannot fasten my seat-belt. Δέν μπορῶ νά δέσω τή ζώνη ἀσφαλείας.

thén boró ná théso tí zóni asfalías

SHIP

The Greek islands cover an area more extensive than mainland Greece itself. They include much of the loveliest scenery and many of the most charming villages of the country, as well as a great number of ancient sites. There are frequent boat services to these islands from Piraeus, the port of Athens. It is wise to find out from a travel agent how long the trip takes and whether it is advisable to book; if you travel during a national holiday, when boats are usually over-booked, you should be at the quayside in good time or you won't get on.

The nearer islands, such as Aegina, Poros, Hydra and Spetsai, have several boats a day. Some are served by "Express", a fast hydrofoil craft rather more expensive than the ordinary services. The farther islands may often be reached by overnight service.

VOCABULARY

anchor, ἡ ἄγκυρα (í ángkira)
below, κάτω (káto)
berth, κρεβάτι (κουκέτα) (kreváti, kookéta)
boat (*open*), ἡ βάρκα (í várka)
bow, ἡ πρῶρα (í próra)
bridge, ἡ γέφυρα (í yéfira)
cabin, ἡ καμπίνα (í kabína)
captain, ὁ καπετάνιος (ó kapetánios)
chain, ἡ ἁλυσίδα (í alisítha)
crane, ὁ γερανός (ó yeranós)
deck, τό κατάστρωμα (tó katástroma)
deck-chair, ἡ σαἰζ-λόνγκ (í shéz-lóng)
dining-room, ἡ τραπεζαρία (í trapezaría)
disembark, to, ἀποβιβάζομαι (apovivázome)

SHIP

dormitory-class, ντορμιτόρυ (dormitóry)
embark, to, ἐπιβιβάζομαι (epivivázome)
engine-room, τό μηχανοστάσιο (tó mihanostásio)
first-class, ἡ πρώτη θέση (í próti thési)
funnel, τό φουγάρο (tó foogháro)
gangway, ἡ σκάλα (í skála)
harbour, τό λιμάνι (tó limáni)
hold, τό ἀμπάρι (tó abári)
island, τό νησί (tó nisí)
lifebelt, τό σωσίβιο (tó sosívio)
lifeboat, ἡ λέμβος (í lémvos)
mast, τό κατάρτι (tó katárti)
port, τό λιμάνι (tó limáni)
porthole, τό φινιστρίνι (tó finistríni)
purser, ὁ ἀρχικαμαρῶτος (ó arhikamarótos)
quay, ἡ προκυμαία (í prokiméa)
sailor, ὁ ναύτης (ó náftis)
sea, ἡ θάλασσα (í thálasa)
second class, ἡ δευτέρα θέσις (í theftéra thésis)
ship, τό πλοῖον (to plíon)
smoke, soot, ὁ καπνός, ἡ καπνιά (ó kapnós, í kapnyá)
stern, ἡ πρύμη (í prími)
steward, ὁ καμαρῶτος (ó kamarótos)
storm, ἡ θύελλα (í thíela)
tourist, ὁ τουρίστας (ó tourístas)
tourist class, ἡ τουριστική θέσις (í tooristikí thésis)
wave, τό κῦμα (tó kíma)
winch, τό βίντσι (tó víntsi)
wind, ὁ ἄνεμος (ó ánemos)

Is there a ship on Monday for Rhodes? Ὑπάρχει πλοῖο τή Δευτέρα γιά τή Ρόδο;
ipárhi plío tí theftéra yá tí Rótho?

What time does it sail? Τί ὥρα φεύγει;
tí óra févyi?

How long does the journey take? Πόσο κρατάει τό ταξίδι;
póso kratái tó taksíthi?

Please book me two places in the first- (second, tourist) class. Παρακαλῶ θέλω νά κλείσω δύο θέσεις πρώτης (δευτέρας, τουριστικῆς) θέσης.
parakaló thélo ná klíso thío thésis prótis (theftéras, tooristikís) thésis

I want a cabin to myself. Θέλω καμπίνα μόνος μου.
thélo kabína mónosmoo

How many berths are there   Πόσα κρεβάτια ὑπάρχουν στήν
in the cabin?   καμπίνα;
          pósa krevátia ipárhoon stín kabína?

Does this include all meals?   Περιέχονται σ'αὐτό καί ὅλα τά
                               γεύματα;
          periéhonde saftó ké óla tá yévmata?

How much does it cost?   Πόσο κάνει;
          póso káni?

Can you give me a reduction?   Μπορεῖτε νά μοῦ κάνετε ἔκπτω-
                                   ση;
          boríte ná moó kánete ékptosi?

I want to travel deck.   Θέλω νά ταξιδεύσω κατά-
                                 στρωμα.
          thélo ná taksithéfso katástroma

Should I book my return   Νά κλείσω μετ'ἐπιστροφῆς τώρα;
passage now?
          ná klíso metepistrofís tóra?

What is the name of the   Πῶς λέγεται τό πλοῖο;
ship?
          pós léyete tó plío?

Where does it sail from?   'Από ποῦ ξεκινάει;
          apó poó ksekinái?

Does the ship carry cars?   Μεταφέρει τό πλοῖο αὐτοκίνητα;
          metaféri tó plío aftokínita?

How much does it cost to   Πόσο κάνει ἡ μεταφορά αὐτο-
take a car from Piraeus to   κινήτου ἀπό τόν Πειραιᾶ στό
Herakleion?   Ἡράκλειο;
      póso káni í metaforá aftokinítoo apó tón Pireá stó Iráklio?

Will it be crowded?   Θά εἶναι γεμᾶτο;
          thá íne yemáto?

Will it be rough?   Θά ἔχει θάλασσα;
          thá éhi thálasa?

Where is the Purser's office?   Ποῦ εἶναι τό γραφεῖο τοῦ
                               ἀρχικαμαρώτου;
          poó íne tó ghrafío toó arhikamarótoo?

Can you find me a better berth (cabin) please?

Μπορεῖτε νά μοῦ βρῆτε καλύτερο κρεβάτι (καλύτερη καμπίνα), παρακαλῶ;

boríte ná moó vríte kalítero kreváti (kalíteri kabína) parakaló?

The sheets are dirty.

Τά σεντόνια εἶναι βρώμικα.

tá sendónia íne vrómika

Please close the porthole.

Παρακαλῶ κλεῖστε τό φινιστρίνι.

parakaló klíste tó finistríni

Where is the toilet?

Ποῦ εἶναι ἡ τουαλέττα;

poó íne í tooaléta?

Where are we now?

Ποῦ βρισκόμαστε τώρα;

poó vriskómaste tóra?

Do we call at Tinos?

Θά σταματήσωμε στήν Τῆνο;

thá stamatísome stín Tíno?

How long do we stay?

Πόσο θά μείνωμε;

póso thá mínome?

Can we go ashore?

Μποροῦμε νά κατεβοῦμε;

boroóme ná katevoóme?

The ship doesn't enter the harbour.

Τό πλοῖο δέν μπαίνει στό λιμάνι.

tó plío thén béni stó limáni

You disembark in small boats.

Θά βγῆτε μέ βάρκες.

thá vyíte mé várkes

Where is the gangway?

Ποῦ εἶναι ἡ σκάλα;

poó íne í skála?

Please don't push.

Παρακαλῶ μή σπρώχνετε.

parakaló mí spróhnete

Where is the shipping agent's office?

Ποῦ βρίσκεται τό πρακτορεῖο τοῦ πλοίου;

poó vrískete tó praktorío toó plíoo?

COACH, BUS, TAXI AND UNDERGROUND RAILWAY

Many travel agencies run tours all over Greece in fairly luxurious coaches called "pullman". Otherwise, inter-city buses are often crowded and uncomfortable; however they are cheap and interesting. The bus system in Athens and Piraeus is complicated because the cities are so large and sprawling. Most buses travel between the city centre and one of the suburbs; one or two lines, notably the trolley-buses, cross the centre of Athens (i.e. Omonia Square or thereabouts). Fare stages are longer than is usual in England; in fact for journeys of any length up to a mile or so from the centre of Athens there is usually one fixed fare. On the lines mentioned above a **double** or **"continuation" ticket,** συνέχεια (sinéhia), entitles the passenger to stay on the bus after it has crossed the city centre.

Children below the age of four travel free: all others pay full fare.

Smoking is strictly forbidden in all buses.

Taxis are plentiful, and in Athens most have an illuminated sign saying "taxi" on the roof. They have meters like London taxis; a short journey in the city centre averages around ten drachmas (2s. 6d.). In general, taxi-drivers do not expect a tip. In the country or for any long journey it is as well to agree upon the fare before setting out.

There is an **electric railway** (ὁ ἠλεκτρικός, o ilektrikós), running for part of its length underground, joining Piraeus with the centre of Athens (Omonia Square) and continuing through certain northern suburbs to Kifissia.

VOCABULARY

bus, τό λεωφορεῖο (tó leoforío)
coach, τό πούλμαν (tó poólman)
conductor, ὁ εἰσπράκτορας (ó ispráktoras)
continuation ticket, ἡ συνέχεια (í sinéhya)
driver, ὁ ὁδηγός (ó othighós)
fare, τά ναῦλα (tá návla)
inside, μέσα (mésa)
inspector, ὁ ἐλεγκτής (ó elengktís)
passenger, ὁ ἐπιβάτης (ó epivátis)
station, ὁ σταθμός (ó stathmós)
stop, ἡ στάσις (í stásis)
taxi, τό ταξί (tó taksí)
taxi-rank, ὁ σταθμός ταξί (ó stathmós taksí)
ticket, τό εἰσιτήριο (tó isitírio)
tram, τό τράμ (tó trám)
trolley-bus, τό τρόλλεϋ (tó tróley)
underground train, ὁ ἠλεκτρικός (ó ilektrikós)

Where can one find a bus Ποῦ θά πάρω τό λεωφορεῖο
for . . .?   γιά . . .;
                    poó thá páro tó leoforío yá . . .?

Does this bus go to . . .? Πάει στό . . .;
pái sto . . .?

Is this the stop for . . .? Εἶναι αὐτή ἡ στάση γιά . . .;
íne aftí í stási yá . . .?

Are you going to . . .? Πάει στό . . .;
pái stó . . .?

I want to get off at . . . Θέλω νά κατέβω στό . . .
thélo ná katévo stó . . .

At the next stop. Στήν ἄλλη στάση.
stín áli stási

Do you pass . . .? Περνάει ἀπό . . .;
pernái apó . . .?

Do you go near . . .? Περνάει κοντά . . .;
pernái kondá . . .?

Will you tell me when we get there, please? Μπορεῖτε νά μοῦ πῆτε ὅταν θά φθάσωμε ἐκεῖ, παρακαλῶ;
boríte ná moó píte ótan thá fthásome ekí, parakaló

Call me a taxi. Μοῦ φωνάζετε ἕνα ταξί;
moó fonázete éna taksí?

I want a quick look round the town. Θέλω ἕνα σύντομο γύρο τῆς πόλης.
thélo éna síndomo yíro tís pólis

We want to tour the main streets. Θέλουμε νά δοῦμε τούς κεντρικούς δρόμους.
théloome ná thoóme toós kendrikoós thrómoos

Take us round the principal monuments. Νά μᾶς πᾶτε στά κυριώτερα μνημεῖα.
ná más páte stá kiriótera mnimía

Go quickly, I am in a great hurry. Πήγαινε γρήγορα. Βιάζομαι πολύ.
píyene ghríghora.   viázome polí

Please wait here for a few minutes. Περιμένετε ἐδῶ, παρακαλῶ, λίγα λεπτά.
periménete ethó, parakaló, lígha leptá

Can I take this suitcase (bag, rucksack) with me inside? Μπορῶ νά πάρω αὐτή τή βαλίτσα (σάκκο, σακκίδιο) μέσα;
boró ná páro aftí tí valítsa (sáko, sakíthyo) mésa?

No, it will have to go on the roof. Ὄχι, πρέπει νά πάη ἐπάνω.

óhi, prépi ná pái epáno

Please get my suitcase down. Παρακαλῶ κατεβᾶστε τίς βαλίτσες μου.

parakaló kateváste tís valítsesmoo

Stop! I want to get off here. Στάσου. Θέλω νά βγῶ ἐδῶ.

stásoo.   thélo ná vghó ethó

YACHTING
VOCABULARY
(see also p. 68, SHIP.)

aft, πίσω (píso)
aground, καθισμένον, προσηραγμένον (kathizménon, prosiraghménon)
alongside, δίπλα (thípla)
anchor, ἡ ἄγκυρα (í ángkira)
anchor, to, ἀγκυροβολῶ (angkirovoló)
bilge, ἡ σεντίνα (í sendína)
block, ὁ μακαρᾶς, τό παλάγγο, ἡ τροχαλία (ó makarás, tó palángo, í trohalía)
boat (*smallish*), ἡ βάρκα (í várka)
boatbuilder's yard, τό ναυπηγεῖο, ὁ ταρσανᾶς (tó nafpiyío, ó tarsanás)
bollard, ἡ δέστρα (í théstra)
bow, ἡ πρώρα, ἡ πλώρη (í próra, í plóri)
buoy, ἡ σημαδοῦρα (í simathoóra)
cabin, ἡ καμπίνα (í kabína)
caique, τό καΐκι (tó ka-íki)
crew, τό πλήρωμα (tó plíroma)
crew-list, ἡ κατάστασις τοῦ πληρώματος (í katástasis toó plirómatos)
Customs, τό Τελωνεῖον (tó teloníon)
deck (*of a small yacht*), ἡ κουβέρτα (i koovérta)
diesel fuel, τό πετρέλαιο (tó petréleo)
dinghy, τό βαρκάκι (tó varkáki)
engine (*and see under* MOTORING), ἡ μηχανή (i mihaní)
forward, μπροστά (brostá)
gas (*bottled*), τό ὑγρό γκάζι (tó ighró gázi)
harbour, τό λιμάνι (tó limáni)
harbour authorities, τό Λιμεναρχεῖο (tó limenarhío)
hatch, ἡ καταπακτή (í katapaktí)
hatch-cover, τό καπάκι (tó kapáki)
hull, τό σκάφος (tó skáfos)
keel, ἡ καρίνα (í karína)
lifebelt, τό σωσίβιο (tó sosívyo)

lights, τά φανάρια (tá fanárya)
mast, τό ἄλμπουρο, τό κατάρτι (tó álbooro, tó katárti)
mole, ὁ μῶλος (ó mólos)
moor, to, ὁρμίζω (ormízo)
moorings, ἡ ρεμέντζα, ἡ τσαμαδούρα (í reméndza, í tsamathoóra)
motor-boat, ἡ βενζινάκατος (í venzinákatos)
paraffin, τό πετρέλαιο (καθαρό) (tó petréleo katharó)
plank, τό σανίδι (tó saníthi)
port (*harbour*), τό λιμάνι (tó limáni)
port (*left*), ἀριστερά (aristerá)
propeller, ἡ προπέλα (í propéla)
quay, ἡ προκυμαία (í prokiméa)
radio, τό ραδιόφωνο (tó rathiófono)
rock, ὁ βράχος (ó vráhos)
rudder, τό τιμόνι (tó timóni)
sail, τό πανί (tó paní)
ship, τό πλοῖο (tó plío)
slipway, τό καρνάγιο (tó karnáyo)
starboard, δεξιά (theksyá)
stern, ἡ πρύμη (í prími)
stores, τά ἐφόδια (tá efóthya)
storm, ἡ θύελλα (í thíela)
tiller, τό τιμόνι (tó timóni)
tug, τό ρεμοῦλκο (tó remoólko)
warp, ἡ ρεμέζα (í reméza)
wave, τό κῦμα (tó kíma)
weather-forecast, τό δελτίον καιροῦ (tó theltíon keroó)
wheel, τό τιμόνι (tó timóni)
wind, ὁ ἀέρας, ὁ ἄνεμος (ó aéras, ó ánemos)
wire-rope, τό συρματάκι (tó sirmatáki)
wreck, τό ναυάγιο (tó naváyo)
yacht, τό κόττερο, τό γιότ (tó kótero, tó yót)

Heave!	Τράβα! tráva!
Pay out!	Λάσκα! láska!
Stop!	Ὄπα! ópa!
Cast off!	Λύσε! líse!
Can I berth here?	Μπορῶ νά ρεμετζάρω; boró ná remendzáro?
Can I come alongside?	Μπορῶ νά πέσω δίπλα; boró ná péso thípla?

Where is the harbour-master's office? Ποῦ εἶναι τό Λιμεναρχεῖο;

poó íne tó limenarhío

Where have you come from? Ἀπό ποῦ ἔρχεστε;

apó poó érheste?

How long are you staying? Πόσο θά μείνετε;

póso thá mínete?

Here is the crew-list. Νά ἡ κατάστασις πληρώματος.

ná í katástasis plirómatos

Where can I get stores? Ποῦ μπορῶ ν'ἀνεφοδιαστῶ;

poó boró nanefothyastó?

Can I get duty-free fuel? Μπορῶ νά πάρω τράνζιτο πετρέλαιο;

boró ná páro tránzito petréleo?

Can water be pumped aboard? Ἔχει σωληνάκι γιά νερό;

éhi solináki yá neró?

Is it deep enough for us? Ἔχει νερά;

éhi nerá?

HOTELS

In Greece hotels are graded according to quality, and charges are fixed by law. The list of charges, usually printed in Greek, English and French, must be displayed in all hotel bedrooms.

A number of "tourist hotels" or ksenias, which are more luxurious and a little more expensive than the ordinary hotels, have been built at strategic spots.

In many small but much-frequented towns, such as Delphi or Nafplion, accommodation may often be found in private houses if all the hotels are full. Enquiry at the cafe, in a shop or of a Tourist policeman will produce addresses. Charges are usually slightly less than at a hotel.

The best way to book a hotel is to get a travel agent to telephone, though at all the larger hotels English is understood.

VOCABULARY

air-conditioning, ξαρ κοντίσιον (éar kondísion)
armchair, ἡ πολυθρόνα (í polithróna)
bath, ἡ μπανιέρα (í banyéra)
bathroom, τό μπάνιο (tó bányo)
bed, τό κρεβάτι (tó kreváti)
bedspread, τό σκέπασμα (tó sképazma)

bedroom, ἡ κρεβατοκάμαρα (í krevatokámara)
   single, κρεβατοκάμαρα μονή (krevatokámara moní)
   double, κρεβατοκάμαρα διπλή (krevatokámara thiplí)
   with twin beds, κρεβατοκάμαρα μέ δύο κρεβάτια
   with a double bed, κρεβατοκάμαρα μέ διπλό κρεβάτι
bell, τό κουδοῦνι (tó koothoóni)
bill, ὁ λογαριασμός (ó loghariazmós)
blanket, ἡ κουβέρτα (í koovérta)
blind, τό σκοῦρο (tó skoóro)
breakfast, τό πρόγευμα (tó próyevma)
boarding-house, ἡ πανσιόν (í pansyón)
bolster, ἡ μαξιλάρα (í maksilára)
bulb, ὁ γλόμπος (ó ghlómbos)
central heating, τό καλοριφέρ (tó kalorifér)
chair, ἡ καρέκλα (í karékla)
chambermaid, ἡ καμαριέρα (í kamaryéra)
coat-hanger, ἡ κρεμάστρα (í kremástra)
complaint, τό παράπονο (tó parápono)
cook, ὁ μάγειρος (ó máyiros)
cupboard, ἡ ντουλάπα (í doolápa)
curtain, ἡ κουρτίνα (í koortína)
dining room, ἡ τραπεζαρία (í trapezaría)
enquiries, οἱ πληροφορίες (í plirofóries)
floor (*storey*), τό πάτωμα, ὁ ὄροφος (tó pátoma, ó órofos)
floor (*underfoot*), τό πάτωμα (tó pátoma)
hall, τό χώλ (tó hól)
hotel, τό ξενοδοχεῖο (tó ksenothohío)
hotel-keeper, ὁ ξενοδόχος (ó ksenothóhos)
hot-water bottle, ἡ θερμοφόρα (í thermofóra)
key, τό κλειδί (tó klithí)
lavatory, τό ἀποχωρητήριο, ἡ τουαλέτα (tó apohoritírio, í tooaléta)
lift, τό ἀσανσέρ (tó asansér)
lounge, τό σαλόνι (tó salóni)
management, ἡ διαχείρισις (í thiahírisis)
manager, ὁ διαχειριστής (ó thiahiristís)
mattress, τό στρῶμα (tó stróma)
office, τό γραφεῖο (tó ghrafío)
page-boy, ὁ καμαριέρης (ó kamaryéris)
pillow, τό μαξιλάρι (tó maksilári)
plug (*electric*), ἡ πρίζα (í príza)
plug (*wash basin*), τό βούλωμα (tó vóoloma)
porter, ὁ θυρωρός (ó thirorós)
proprietor, ὁ ἰδιοκτήτης (ó ithioktítis)
reception, πληροφορίαι (pliroforíe)
radiator, τό καλοριφέρ (tó kalorifér)
reading-lamp, τό πορτατίφ (tó portatíf)
service, ἡ ὑπηρεσία (í ipiresía)
sheet, τό σεντόνι (tó sendóni)
shelf, τό ράφι (tó ráfi)

shower, τό ντούς (tó doós)
shutter, τό ἐξώφυλλο (tó eksófilo)
sitting-room, τό σαλόνι (tó salóni)
staircase, ἡ σκάλα (í skála)
switch, ὁ διακόπτης (ó thiakóptis)
table, τό τραπέζι (tó trapézi)
tap (hot, cold), ἡ βρύση (θερμό, ψυχρό) (í vrísi (thermó, psihró))
towel, ἡ πετσέτα (í petséta)
tourist hotel, τό τουριστικό ξενοδοχεῖο (tó tooristikó ksenothohío)
wardrobe, ἡ ντουλάπα (í doolápa)
wash-basin, ὁ νιπτήρας (ó niptíras)
window, τό παράθυρο (tó paráthiro)

NOTICES

ΤΟ ΞΕΝΟΔΟΧΕΙΟΝ (ksenothohíon) = **hotel**
ΤΟ ΞΕΝΟΔΟΧΕΙΟΝ ΥΠΝΟΥ (ksenothohíon ípnoo) = **hotel** *that does not
　　serve meals. It should not be assumed that all others do.*
ΤΟ ΠΑΝΔΟΧΕΙΟΝ (panthohíon) = **hotel**, rather lower-grade.
ΣΥΡΑΤΕ (sírate) = **pull**
ΩΘΗΣΑΤΕ (othísate) = **push**
ΘΕΡΜΟ (thermó) = **hot**
ΨΥΧΡΟ (psihró) = **cold**

LAUNDRY AND CLEANING

belt, ἡ ζώνη (í zóni)
brassiere, τό σουτιέν (tó sootyén)
button, τό κουμπί (tó koombí)
clothes, τά ροῦχα (tá roóha)
collar, τό κολάρο (tó koláro)
handkerchief, τό μαντῆλι (tó mandíli)
jacket, ἡ ζακέτα (í zakéta)
jumper, τό σακάκι (tó sakáki)
nightdress, τό νυχτικό (tó nihtikó)
pants, τό παντελόνι (tó pandelóni)
panties, ἡ κυλότα (í kilóta)
petticoat, τό μεσοφόρι (tó mesofóri)
pullover, τό πουλόβερ (tó poolóver)
pyjamas, οἱ πυτζάμες (í pitzámes)
scarf, τό κασκόλ (tó kaskól)
shirt, τό πουκάμισο (tó pookámiso)
shoes, τά παπούτσια (tá papoótsya)
slip, τό κομπιναιζόν (tó kombinezón)
socks, οἱ κάλτσες (í káltses)
stockings, οἱ κάλτσες (γυναικεῖες) (í káltses (yinekíes))
suit, τό κοστοῦμι (tó kostoómi)
suspender belt, girdle, οἱ ζαρτιέρες (í zartiéres)
trousers, τό παντελόνι (tó pandelóni)
zip-fastener, τό ἐκλαίρ (tó eklér)
skirt, ἡ φούστα (í foósta)

blouse, ἡ μπλούζα (í blóóza)
dress, τό φόρεμα (tó fórema)

Where is the office?	Ποῦ εἶναι τό γραφεῖο;
	poó íne tó ghrafío?
I am Mr. (Mrs., Miss) . . .	Εἶμαι ὁ κύριος (κυρία, δεσποινίς) . . .
	íme ó kírios (kiría, thespinís) . . .
I wrote to you.	Σᾶς ἔγραψα.
	sás éghrapsa
I telephoned you.	Σᾶς τηλεφώνησα.
	sás tilefónisa
Did you get my letter?	Δέν πήρατε τό γράμμα μου;
	thén pírate tó ghrámamoo?
I asked for a room on the first (second) floor.	Ζήτησα ἕνα δωμάτιο στό πρῶτο (δεύτερο) πάτωμα.
	zítisa éna thomátio stó próto (théftero) pátoma
Can I have a room for the night?	Μπορῶ νά ἔχω ἕνα δωμάτιο γιά ἀπόψε;
	boró náého éna thomátio yá apópse?
I shall stay one night (two, three, four nights, weeks).	Θά μείνω μιά νύχτα (δύο, τρεῖς, τέσσερες νύχτες, ἑβδομάδες)
	thá míno miá níhta (thío, trís, téseres níhtes, evthomáthes
I am staying for only two or three days.	Θά μείνω μόνο δύο ἤ τρεῖς ἡμέρες.
	thá míno móno thío í trís iméres
I want a room for myself only.	Θέλω δωμάτιο γιά μένα μόνο.
	thélo thomátio yá ména móno
I want a room with two beds (a double bed).	Θέλω δωμάτιο μέ δυό κρεβάτια (διπλό κρεβάτι).
	thélo thomátio mé thío kreváttia (tiplό krevάti)
Have you got one on the first floor (ground floor)?	Ἔχετε ἕνα στόν πρῶτο ὄροφο (στό ἰσόγειο);
	éhete éna stón próto órofo (stó isóyo?)
Have you a room with a private bathroom?	Ἔχετε δωμάτιο μέ ἰδιαίτερο μπάνιο;
	éhete thomátio mé ithiétero bányo?

Is there a lift?	Ὑπάρχει ἀσανσέρ; ipárhi asansér?
What is the price of a room per night?	Πόσο ἔχει τό δωμάτιο γιά μιά νύχτα; póso éhi tó thomátio yá miá níhta?
How much do you charge per day (per week) including meals?	Πόσο τό χρεώνετε τή μέρα (τήν ἑβδομάδα) μαζί μέ τά γεύματα; póso tó hreónete tí méra (tín evthomátha) mazí mé tá yévmata?
I want a bedroom with breakfast only.	Θέλω δωμάτιο μέ πρόγευμα μόνο. thélo thomátio mé próyevma móno
Can I see the room?	Μπορῶ νά δῶ τό δωμάτιο; boró ná thó tó thomátio?
Have you nothing better?	Δέν ἔχει τίποτα καλύτερο; thén éhi típota kalítero?
I want a quiet room.	Θέλω ἕνα ἥσυχο δωμάτιο. thélo éna ísiho thomátio
I cannot sleep in this room; there is too much noise.	Δέν μπορῶ νά κοιμηθῶ σ'αὐτό τό δωμάτιο. Ἔχει πολύ θόρυβο. thén boró ná kimithó saftó tó thomátio. éhi polí thórivo
Have you a room looking on to the sea (the garden, the square)?	Ἔχετε δωμάτιο μέ θέα τή θάλασσα (τόν κῆπο, τήν πλατεῖα); éhete thomátio mé théa tí thálasa (tón kípo, tín platía)?
Have you nothing cheaper?	Δέν ἔχετε τίποτα φθηνότερο; thén éhete típota fthinótero?
I do not like my room.	Δέν μοῦ ἀρέσει τό δωμάτιό μου. thén moó arési tó thomátiómoo
Can you give me a room on another floor?	Μπορεῖτε νά μοῦ δώσετε ἕνα δωμάτιο σ'ἄλλον ὄροφο; boríte ná moó thósete éna thomátio sálon órofo?
I do not want a room looking on to the street.	Δέν θέλω δωμάτιο μέ θέα στό δρόμο. thén thélo thomátio mé théa stó thrómo

The noise prevents me from sleeping.	Ὁ θόρυβος μέ ἐμποδίζει νά κοιμηθῶ.

ó thórivos mé embothízi ná kimithó

If you cannot give me something better I shall have to look elsewhere.	Ἄν δέν μπορεῖτε νά μοῦ δώσετε κάτι καλύτερο θά πρέπει νά κυττάξω ἀλλοῦ.

án thén boríte ná moó thósete káti kalítero thá prépi ná kitákso aloó

Very well, I shall take this room.	Πολύ καλά, θά πάρω τό δωμάτιο.

polí kalá, thá páro tó thomátio

Have my luggage taken up, please.	Μοῦ στέλνετε τίς βαλίτσες μου ἐπάνω, παρακαλῶ.

moó stélnete tís valítsesmoo epáno, parakaló

Wake me at seven a.m.	Ξυπνῆστε με στίς ἑπτά τό πρωΐ.

ksipnísteme stís eptá tó pro-í

I have missed my train.	Ἔχασα τό τραῖνο μου.

éhasa tó trénomoo

Where can I spend the night?	Ποῦ μπορῶ νά περάσω τή νύχτα;

poó boró ná peráso tí níhta ?

I shall have to stay here overnight.	Θά πρέπει νά μείνω ἐδῶ τή νύχτα.

thá prépi ná míno ethó tí níhta

Can you put me up for the night?	Μπορεῖτε νά μέ βολέψετε γιά ἀπόψε;

boríte ná mé volépsete yá apópse ?

Any room will do.	Ὅ,τι δωμάτιο νἆναι.

óti thomátio náne

I shall pay in advance.	Θά πληρώσω προκαταβολικῶς.

thá pliróso prokatavolikós

I have no luggage.	Δέν ἔχω ἀποσκευές.

thén ého aposkevés

Can you recommend a small hotel?	Μπορεῖτε νά μοῦ συστήσετε κανένα μικρό ξενοδοχεῖο;

boríte ná moó sistísete kanéna mikró ksenothohío ?

| Is there a house where we can stay? | Ὑπάρχει κανένα σπίτι νά μείνουμε; |
| | ipárhi kanéna spíti ná mínoome? |

| Can you recommend a good restaurant? | Μπορεῖτε νά μοῦ συστήσετε ἕνα καλό ἑστιατόριο; |
| | boríte ná moó sistísete éna kaló estiatório? |

| Are there any letters for me? | Ὑπάρχουν γράμματα γιά μένα; |
| | ipárhoon ghrámata yá ména? |

| I am expecting a gentleman (a lady). | Περιμένω ἕναν κύριο (μιά κυρία). |
| | periméno éna kírio (miá kiría) |

| Please send him (her) up at once. | Παρακαλῶ στεῖλτε τον (την) ἐπάνω ἀμέσως. |
| | parakaló stílteton (tin) epáno amésos |

| If anyone asks for me, please tell them to wait. | Ἄν μέ ζητήση κανείς, παρακαλῶ πέστε νά περιμένη. |
| | án mé zitísi kanís, parakaló péste ná periméni |

| I am going out. | Θά βγῶ. |
| | thá vghó |

| I shall be back at three. | Θά γυρίσω στίς τρεῖς. |
| | thá yiríso stís trís |

| Someone telephoned you. | Κάποιος σᾶς τηλεφώνησε. |
| | kápyos sás tilefónise |

| They asked you to ring this number. | Εἶπαν νά πάρετε αὐτόν τόν ἀριθμό. |
| | ípan ná párete aftón tón arithmó |

| Will you get this number for me, please. | Μοῦ παίρνετε αὐτόν τόν ἀριθμό; |
| | moó pérnete aftón tón arithmó? |

| The chambermaid never comes when I ring. | Ἡ καμαριέρα δέν ἀνεβαίνει ποτέ ὅταν χτυπῶ. |
| | í kamaryéra thén anevéni poté ótan htipó |

| Are you the chambermaid? | Εἴσαστε ἡ καμαριέρα; |
| | ísaste í kamaryéra? |

| I have lost ... in my room. | Ἔχασα ... στό δωμάτιό μου. |
| | éhasa ... stó thomátiómoo |

Will you look for it, please. Ψάχνετε σᾶς παρακαλῶ.
psáhnete, sás parakaló

I should like some iced water. Θά ἤθελα λίγο παγωμένο νερό.
thá íthela lígho paghoméno neró

Please bring me a bottle of mineral water. Μοῦ δίνετε παρακαλῶ μεταλλικό νερό;
moó thínete parakaló metalikó neró

Can I drink the water from the tap? Τό νερό τῆς βρύσης πίνεται;
tó neró tís vrísis pínete?

Bring me some hot water for shaving, please. Μοῦ δίνετε ζεστό νερό γιά ξύρισμα παρακαλῶ.
moó thínete zestó neró yá ksírizma, parakaló

I should like a hot bath. Θά ἤθελα ἕνα ζεστό μπάνιο.
thá íthela éna zestó bányo

There are no towels in the bathroom. Δέν ὑπάρχουν πετσέτες στό μπάνιο.
thén ipárhoon petsétes stó bányo

Please open (close) the window (the shutters). Ἀνοῖξτε (κλεῖστε) τό παράθυρο (τά παντζούρια) παρακαλῶ.
aníkste (klíste) tó paráthiro (tá pandzoória) parakaló

The sheets on this bed are damp. Τά σεντόνια τοῦ κρεβατιοῦ εἶναι ὑγρά.
tá sendónia toó krevatyoó íne ighrá

This room is not clean. Αὐτό τό δωμάτιο δέν εἶναι καθαρό.
aftó tó thomátio thén íne katharó

May I have a pillow? Μοῦ δίνετε ἕνα μαξιλάρι;
moó thínete éna maksilári?

I should like an extra blanket. Θά ἤθελα ἀκόμα μιά κουβέρτα.
thá íthela akóma miá koovérta

It is very cold at night. Can you give me a quilt? Κάνει κρύο τή νύχτα. Μοῦ δίνετε ἕνα πάπλωμα;
káni krío tí níhta. moó thínete éna páploma?

Have you made the bed?	Ἔχετε φτιάξει τό κρεβάτι; éhete ftiáksi tó kreváti?
I am going to bed at once.	Θά πέσω ἀμέσως. thá péso amésos
You have not brought the hot water (towel).	Δέν μοῦ φέρατε τό ζεστό νερό (τήν πετσέτα). thén moó férate tó zestó neró (tín petséta)
It is cold (hot) in this room.	Κάνει κρύο (ζέστη) σ'αὐτό τό δωμάτιο. káni krío (zésti) saftó tó thomátio
Can you bring me a hot-water bottle, please.	Μπορεῖτε νά μοῦ δώσετε μιά θερμοφόρα παρακαλῶ. boríte ná moó thósete miá thermofóra parakaló
The radiator isn't working.	Τό καλοριφέρ δέν δουλεύει. tó kalorifér thén thoolévi
The radiator is too hot.	Τό καλοριφέρ εἶναι πολύ ζεστό. tó kalorifér íne polí zestó
The air-conditioning isn't working (is too cold, is very noisy).	Τό ἔαρ κοντίσιον δέν δουλεύει (εἶναι κρύο, κάνει πολύ θό- ρυβο). tó éar kondísion thén thoolévi (íne krío, káni polí thórivo)
The light is very poor.	Τό φῶς εἶναι μικρό. tó fós íne mikró
This bulb is broken.	Ἔσπασε ὁ γλόμπος. éspase ó ghlómbos
Is there a plug for my electric razor?	Ὑπάρχει πρίζα γιά τήν ξυρισ- τική μηχανή μου; ipárhi príza yá tín ksiristikí mihanímoo?
What is the voltage?	Πόσων βόλτ εἶναι τό ρεῦμα; póson vólt íne tó révma?
I have some things to be washed.	Ἔχω μερικά πράγματα γιά πλύσιμο. ého meriká prághmata yá plísimo
Can I have them back today?	Θά εἶναι ἔτοιμα σήμερα; thá íne étima símera?
When will they be ready?	Πότε θά εἶναι ἔτοιμα; póte thá íne étima?

I must have them by Satur- Πρέπει νά τά ἔχω ἕως τό
day (by five o'clock). Σάββατο (ἕως τίς πέντε).
prépi ná tá ého éos tó sávato (éos tís pénde)

There is a button missing. Μοῦ λείπει ἕνα κουμπί.
moó lípi éna koombí

Can you replace it? Μπορεῖτε νά τό ἀντικατασ-
τήσετε;
boríte ná tó andikatastísete?

This zip-fastener is broken. Ἔσπασε τό ἐκλαίρ.
éspase tó eklér

Can it be mended? Μπορεῖ νά διορθωθῆ;
borí ná thiorthothí?

I have two pairs of socks to Ἔχω δύο ζευγάρια κάλτσες γιά
be mended. μπάλωμα.
ého thío zevghária káltses yá báloma

Please have these clothes Στεγνῶστε αὐτά τά ροῦχα
dried. παρακαλῶ.
steghnóste aftá tá roóha parakaló

I shall leave my clothes at Θά ἀφήσω τά ροῦχα μου ἔξω
the door. ἀπ'τήν πόρτα.
thá afíso tá roóhamoo ékso ap tín pórta

Will you have them brushed? Τά δίνετε νά τά ξεσκονίσουν;
tá thínete ná tá kseskonísoon?

Please have these shoes Δίνετε νά μοῦ γυαλίσουν τά
cleaned. παπούτσια;
thínete ná moó yalísoon tá papoótsya?
(*It is not the custom to leave one's shoes outside the door to be cleaned*)

My shoes are damp. Please Τά παπούτσια μου εἶναι βρεγ-
have them dried. μένα. Μπορεῖτε νά μοῦ τά
στεγνώσετε παρακαλῶ.
tá papoótsyamoo íne vreghména. borite ná moó tá steghnósete, parakaló

These shoes are not mine. Τά παπούτσια αὐτά δέν εἶναι
δικά μου.
tá papoótsya aftá thén íne thikámoo

I left my shoes here; where Ἄφησα τά παπούτσια μου
are they? ἐδῶ, ποῦ εἶναι;
áfisa tá papoótsyamoo ethó. poó íne?

Have you seen my ...?　　　Εἴδατε τό ... μου;
　　　　íthate tó ... moo?

Have you any English news-　Ἔχετε ἀγγλικές ἐφημερίδες;
papers?
　　　　éhete anglikés efimeríthes?

Can I have some paper and　Μπορεῖτε νά μοῦ δώσετε λίγο
envelopes, please?　　　χαρτί καί φακέλλους, παρα-
　　　　　　　　　　　καλῶ;
　　　boríte ná moó thósete lígho hartí ké fakéloos, parakaló?

Have you any stamps?　　Ἔχετε γραμματόσημα;
　　　　éhete ghramatósima?

How much does it cost to　Πόσο κοστίζει νά στείλω ἕνα
send a letter (postcard)　γράμμα (κάρτα) στήν Ἀγγ-
to England?　　　　　λία;
　　　póso kostízi ná stílo éna ghráma (miá kárta) stín anglía?

Is there a letter-box nearby?　Ὑπάρχει γραμματοκιβώτιο ἐδῶ
　　　　　　　　　　κοντά;
　　　ipárhi ghramatokivótio ethó kondá?

Where is the post-office?　Ποῦ εἶναι τό ταχυδρομεῖο;
　　　poó íne tó tahythromío?

I want to send a telegram.　Θέλω νά στείλω ἕνα τηλεγρά-
　　　　　　　　　　φημα.
　　　thélo ná stílo éna tileghráfima

I want to telephone.　　Θέλω νά τηλεφωνήσω.
　　　thélo ná tilefoníso

Where can I buy ...?　　Ποῦ μπορῶ ν'ἀγοράσω ...;
　　　poó boró naghoráso ...?

I do not feel well.　I shall　Δέν εἶμαι καλά.　Θά μείνω στό
stay in bed.　　　　　κρεβάτι.
　　　thén íme kalá.　thá míno stó kreváti

Do you know when the　Ξέρετε πότε φεύγουν τά τραῖνα
trains (buses) leave for ...?　(λεωφορεῖα) γιά ...;
　　　ksérete póte févghoon tá tréna (leoforía) yá ...?

Has anyone called to see me?　Μέ ἐζήτησε κανείς;
　　　mé ezítise kanís?

Where should I leave my key? Ποῦ νά ἀφήσω τό κλειδί μου;

poó nafíso tó klithímoo?

What time does the hotel close? Τί ὥρα κλείνει τό ξενοδοχεῖο;

tí óra klíni tó ksenothohío?

Are you open all night? Μένετε ἀνοιχτά ὅλη τή νύχτα;

ménete anihtá óli tí níhta?

There is a draught. Ἔχει ρεῦμα.

éhi révma

Can I have breakfast in my room? Μπορῶ νά πάρω τό πρόγευμα στό δωμάτιό μου;

boró ná páro tó próyevma stó thomatiómoo?

Can we have an English breakfast? Μπορούμε νά ἔχουμε ἀγγλικό πρόγευμα;

boroóme ná éhoome anglikó próyevma?

(Except in the most sophisticated Athenian hotels, you almost certainly cannot; however, there's no harm in asking. It should be possible to get fried or boiled eggs and toast if the hotel is prepared to do any cooking at all, but relatively few of the cheaper hotels provide any meals. You may, however, order Turkish coffee at any time of the day)

Can you put another bed in the room for the child? Μπορεῖτε νά προσθέσετε ἀκόμα ἕνα κρεβάτι γιά τό παιδί μου;

boríte ná prosthésete akóma éna kreváti yá tó pethímoo?

I must leave at once. Πρέπει νά φύγω ἀμέσως.

prépi ná fígho amésos

I have to leave early to-morrow. Πρέπει νά φύγω νωρίς αὔριο.

prépi ná fígho norís ávrio

I shall need a taxi for the station. Θά χρειασθῶ ἕνα ταξί ἕως τό σταθμό.

thá hriasthó éna taksí eós tó stathmó

Order a taxi for 9.30, please. Μοῦ κανονίζετε ἕνα ταξί γιά τίς ἐννέα καί μισή, παρακαλῶ;

moó kanonízete éna taksí yá tís enéa ké misí, parakaló?

I am taking the ... train (bus, aeroplane).
Θά πάρω τό τραῖνο (λεωφο-ρεῖο, τό ἀεροπλάνο) τῶν ...
thá páro tó tréno (tó leoforío, tó aeropláno) tón ...

Please make out the bill.
Παρακαλῶ κάντε μου τόν λο-γαριασμό.
Parakaló, kándemoo tó loghariazmó

I have not enough Greek money.
Δέν ἔχω ἀρκετά Ἑλληνικά χρή-ματα.
thén ého arketá eliniká hrímata

Will you accept a traveller's cheque?
Παίρνετε ταξιδιωτικά τσέκ;
pérnete taksithiotiká tsék?

Will you accept dollars (pounds sterling)?
Παίρνετε δολλάρια (λίρες στερ-λίνες);
pérnete tholária (líres sterlínes?)

Will you have letters sent on to this address, please?
Μοῦ στέλνετε τά γράμματα σ'αὐτή τή διεύθυνση, παρα-καλῶ;
moó stélnete tá ghrámata saftí tí thiéfthinsi, parakalo?

Has the taxi come?
Ἦρθε τό ταξί;
írthe tó taksí?

Fetch another.
Φέρτε μου ἕνα ἄλλο.
fértemoo énálo

Have the luggage brought down.
Πεῖτε νά μοῦ κατεβάσουν τίς βαλίτσες.
píte ná moó katevásoon tís valítses

Put those in the boot.
Βάλτε τις στό πόρτ-μπαγκάζ.
váltetis stó pórt bagáz

I have left ... in my room.
Ξέχασα τό ... στό δωμάτιό μου.
kséhasa ... stó thomatiómoo

Here is the key.
Ὁρίστε τό κλειδί.
oríste tó klithí

Keep this for yourself.
Αὐτό γιά σᾶς.
aftó yá sás

That is all, I think.
Νομίζω πώς τελειώσαμε.
nomízo pós teliósame

I hope you are pleased with the hotel, sir. Ἐλπίζω νά μείνατε εὐχαριστημένος ἀπ'τό Ξενοδοχεῖο, κύριε.

elpízo ná mínate efharistiménos ap tó ksenothohío, kírie

Very pleased indeed. I hope to come again. Πάρα πολύ. Ἐλπίζω νά ξανάρθω.

párapolí. elpízo ná ksanártho

Thank you. Good-bye. Εὐχαριστῶ. Χαίρετε.

efharistó. hérete

SIGHTSEEING AND SEASIDE

It is assumed that the tourist will have a good guide-book and a map of Greece. Street-plans of Athens and Salonica may be bought, or often obtained free from travel-agencies as shipping and air-line hand-outs.

As mentioned before, there are very many coach tours run by different travel-agencies, with English-speaking guides and itineraries ranging from the monuments of Athens to almost the whole of Greece. On such tours one is, of course, bound by the time-table, and they do try to squeeze as many sites as possible into the time.

There are innumerable fine bathing places around the shores of mainland Greece and the islands. In a few places beaches have been enclosed and equipped with cabins, refreshment stalls, lavatories and other amenities; a small charge is made for admission to these beaches or "plages" (πλάζ). In the summer, and especially at weekends, these and also most unenclosed beaches near Athens are very crowded.

Bathing is reasonably safe everywhere, for there are no tides. In places there may be currents, however, and storms with substantial waves can spring up very suddenly. Look out for sea-urchins, which are very painful black prickly balls that grow on rocks. In deeper water, especially in shipping channels, sharks are not uncommon, and swimmers have been eaten.

VOCABULARY

SIGHTSEEING

ancient site, ὁ ἀρχαιολογικός χῶρος (ó arheoloyikós hóros)
anno Domini, A.D. Μετά Χριστόν, μ.Χ. (metá Hristón)
ancient things in general, τά ἀρχαῖα (tá arhéa)
arch, ἡ ἀψίδα (καμάρα) (í apsítha (kamára))
battlement, ἡ ἔπαλξη (í épalksi)
before Christ, B.C. πρό Χριστοῦ, π.Χ. (pró Hristoó)
bridge, ἡ γέφυρα (í yéfira)
building, τό κτίριο (tó ktírio)
carving, τό ἀνάγλυφο (tó anághlifo)
castle, τό κάστρο (tó kástro)
cathedral, ἡ Μητρόπολη (í mitrópoli)

century, ὁ αἰῶνας (ό eónas)
church (Byzantine), ἡ ἐκκλησία (Βυζαντινή) (í eklisía (vizandiní))
coach, τό πούλμαν (tó poólman)
column, ἡ κολώνα (í kolóna)
Corinthian, κορινθιακός (korinthiakós)
Doric, δωρικός (**th**orikós)
epoch, age, ἡ ἐποχή (í epohí)
Frankish, Φράγκικος (frángikos)
gallery, ἡ πινακοθήκη (í pinakothíki)
garden, ὁ κῆπος (ό kípos)
gate, ἡ πύλη (í píli)
grave, ὁ τάφος (ό táfos)
guide, ὁ ξεναγός (ό ksenaghós)
icon, ἡ εἰκόνα (í ikóna)
inscription, ἡ ἐπιγραφή (í epighrafí)
interpreter, ὁ, ἡ διερμηνέας (ό, í **th**ierminéas)
Ionic, Ἰωνικός (ionikós)
Minoan, Μινωϊκός (minoikós)
monument, τό μνημεῖο (tó mnimío)
mosaic, τό μωσαϊκό, τό ψηφιδωτό (tó mosaikó, psifi**th**otó)
museum, τό μουσεῖο (tó moosío)
Mycenaean, Μυκηναϊκός (míkina-ikós)
park, τό πάρκο (tó párko)
pot, τό ἀγγεῖο (tó angío)
potsherd, τό ὄστρακο (tó óstrako)
prehistoric, προϊστορικός (pro-istorikós)
Roman, ρωμαϊκός (roma-íkós)
ruin, τά ἐρείπια (tá erípia)
street, ὁ δρόμὸς (ό **th**rómos)
street-plan, ὁ χάρτης τῆς πόλης (o hártis tís pólis)
square, ἡ πλατεῖα (í platía)
stadium, τό στάδιο (tó stá**th**io)
statue, τό ἄγαλμα (tó ághalma)
style, ὁ ρυθμός (ό rithmós)
temple, ὁ ναός (ό naós)
theatre, τό θέατρο (tó théatro)
tomb, τό μνημεῖο, ὁ τύμβος (tó mnimío, ó tímvos)
Turkish, Τουρκικός (toorkikós)
Venetian, Ἑνετικός (enetikós)
vase, τό βάзο (ἀγγεῖο) (tó vázo, angío)
wall, τό τεῖχος (tó tíhos)

SEASIDE

air-mattress, τό ἀερόστρωμα (to aeróstroma)
bait, τό δόλωμα (tó **th**óloma)
ball, ἡ μπάλλα (í bála)
bathe, to, κάνω μπάνιο (káno bányo)
bathing-cap, ἡ σκούφια (í skoófya)
bathing-costume, τό μαγιό (tó mayó)

bathing hut, ἡ καμπίνα (í kabína)
bay, ὁ κόλπος (ó kólpos)
beach (*with charge for admission*), ἡ πλάζ (í pláz)
beach, natural, ἡ ἀμμουδιά (í amoothyá)
boat, ἡ βάρκα (í várka)
buoy, ἡ σημαδούρα (í simathoóra)
canoe, τό κανώ (tó kanó)
coast, ἡ παραλία (í paralía)
current, τό ρεῦμα (tó révma)
deck-chair, ἡ σαίζ-λόγκ (í séz-lóng)
diving-board, ὁ ἀναβατήρας (ó anavatíras)
excursion, ἡ ἐκδρομή (í ekthromí)
fish, τό ψάρι (tó psári)
fish, to, ψαρεύω (psarévo)
fishing-line, ἡ πετονιά (í petonyá)
flippers (*rubber*), τά βατραχοπέδιλα (tá vatrahopéthila)
goggles, τά γυαλιά (tá yalyá)
harpoon-gun, τό ψαροτούφεκο (tó psarotoófeko)
hook, τό ἀγκίστρι (tó angkístri)
jelly-fish, ἡ τσούχτρα (í tsoóhtra)
lake, ἡ λίμνη (í límni)
lighthouse, ὁ φάρος (ó fáros)
net, τό δίχτυ (tó thíhti)
pebble, τό βότσαλο (tó vótsalo)
raft, ἡ σχεδία (í skhethía)
rock, ὁ βράχος (ó vráhos)
rubber ring, animal, etc., τό σωσίβιο (tó sosívio)
sand, ἡ ἄμμος (í ámos)
sands, ἡ ἀμμουδιά (í amoothyá)
sea, ἡ θάλασσα (í thálasa)
sea-urchin, ὁ ἀχινός (ó ahinós)
seaweed, τό φύκι (tó fíki)
shade (*of tree, etc.*), ἡ σκιά (í skyá)
shark, ὁ καρχαρίας (ó karharías)
shell, τό ὄστρακο (tó óstrako)
shingle, τό χαλίκι (tó halíki)
shore, ἡ ἀκρογιαλιά (í akroyalyá)
shower, τό ντούς (tó doós)
sun, ὁ ἥλιος (ó ílyos)
sunshade, ἡ τέντα (í ténda)
swim, to, κολυμπάω (kolimbáo)
swimming-pool, ἡ πισίνα (í pisína)
towel, ἡ πετσέτα (í petséta)
wave, τό κῦμα (tó kíma)

Have you a list of excur- Ἔχετε πρόγραμμα ἐκδρομῶν;
sions?

        éhete próghrama ekthromón?

How much is this excursion? Πόσο κοστίζει αὐτή ἡ ἐκδρομή;

póso kostízi aftí i ekthromí?

I want two seats for the excursion to . . . Θέλω δυό θέσεις γιά τήν ἐκδρομή στό . . .

thélo thió thésis yá tín ekthromí stó . . .

We want to be together. Θέλουμε νἅμαστε μαζί.

théloome vámaste mazí

I want a guide who speaks English. Θέλω ἕνα ξεναγό πού νά μιλάη ἀγγλικά.

thélo éna ksenaghó poó ná milái anliká

How much should one pay the guide? Πόσο παίρνει ὁ (ἡ) ξεναγός;

póso pérni ó (i) ksenaghós?

We don't need a guide. Δέν χρειαζόμαστε ξεναγό.

thén hriazómaste ksenaghó

That's the end of the tour. Αὐτό εἶναι τό τέλος τῆς περιήγησης.

aftó íne tó télos tís peri-íyisis

Where can I get tickets? Ποῦ μπορῶ νά βρῶ εἰσιτήρια;

poó boró ná vró isitíria?

Is this the right road for . . . ? Εἶναι αὐτός ὁ σωστός δρόμος γιά . . . ;

íne aftós ó sostós thrómos yá . . . ?

What is this building (street)? Τί εἶναι αὐτό τό κτίριο (αὐτός ὁ δρόμος);

tí íne aftó tó ktírio (aftós ó thrómos)?

How far is it from here to . . . ? Πόσο μακρυά εἶναι τό . . . ;

póso makryá íne tó . . . ?

Can one go on foot? Μπορεῖ νά πάη κανείς μέ τά πόδια;

borí ná pái kanís mé tá pódhya?

Can I hire a bicycle (donkey, horse)? Μπορῶ νά νοικιάσω ποδήλατο (γάϊδαρο, ἄλογο);

boró ná nikiáso pothílato (gháitharo, álogho)?

Is there a boy who can show me the way? Εἶναι κανένα παιδί νά μοῦ δείξη τό δρόμο;

íne kanéna pethí ná moó thíksi tó thrómo?

Ought one to take the bus?	Πρέπει νά πάρη κανείς τό αὐτοκίνητο;
	prépi ná pári kanís tó aftokínito?
Is it near (far)?	Εἶναι κοντά (μακρυά);
	íne kondá (makryá)?
Which way?	Ποιό δρόμο;
	pyó thrómo?
Straight on.	Ἴσια.
	ísya
Turn left (right).	Στρίψε ἀριστερά (δεξιά).
	strípse aristerá (theksyá)
Go on till you get to the square.	Προχωρεῖστε ὥσπου νά φθάσετε στήν πλατεῖα.
	prohoríste óspou vá fthásete stín platía
The first (second, third) on the right.	Τό πρῶτο (δεύτερο, τρίτο) δεξιά.
	tó próto (théftero, tríto) theksyá
This way. That way.	Ἀπ'ἐδῶ. Ἀπ'ἐκεῖ.
	apothó. apekí
I was looking for ... and I took the wrong road.	Ἔψαχνα γιά τό ... καί δέν πῆρα τό σωστό δρόμο.
	épsahna yá tó ... ké thén píra tó sostó thrómo
I am lost.	Χάθηκα.
	háthika
What is the name of this church?	Πῶς λέγεται αὐτή ἡ ἐκκλησία;
	pós léyete aftí í eklisía?
What is that ruin (wall, column, arch)?	Τί εἶναι αὐτό τό ἐρείπιο (τεῖχος, κολῶνα, ἀψίδα);
	tí íne aftó tó erípyo (tíhos, kolóna, apsítha)?
Is it ancient?	Εἶναι ἀρχαῖο;
	íne arhéo?
Where is the museum (temple, theatre), please?	Ποῦ εἶναι τό μουσεῖο (ναός, θέατρο) παρακαλῶ;
	poó íne tó moosío (naós, théatro) parakaló?
Is it open?	Εἶναι ἀνοιχτό;
	íne anihtó?

Can we go in? Μπορούμε νά μπούμε;
boroóme ná boóme?

How much does it cost to go Πόσο κοστίζει ἡ εἴσοδος;
in?
póso kostízi í ísothos?

Admission free on Sundays Κυριακή καί Πέμπτη ἡ εἴσοδος
and Thursdays. ἐλευθέρα.
kiriakí ké pémti í ísothos elefthéra

May I take photographs? Μπορῶ νά πάρω φωτογραφίες;
boró ná páro fotoghrafíes?

Have you any postcards? Ἔχετε κάρτες;
éhete kártes?

Have you a map (plan)? Ἔχετε χάρτη (σχεδιάγραμμα);
éhete hartí (skhethyághrama)?

Does this street go to the Πάει αὐτός ὁ δρόμος στήν
Acropolis? Ἀκρόπολη;
pái aftós ó thrómos stín akrópoli?

Where can we bathe? Ποῦ μπορούμε νά κολυμπή-
σουμε;
poó boroóme ná kolimbísoome?

Is there a sandy beach near Ὑπάρχει καμμιά ἀμμουδιά ἐδῶ
here? κοντά;
ipárhi kamyá amoothyá ethó kondá?

Is the water clean? Εἶναι τό νερό καθαρό;
íne tó neró katharó?

I want to take a cabin. How Θέλω καμπίνα. Πόσο κάνει;
much is it?
thélo kabína. póso káni?

Is there a tap anywhere Ὑπάρχει βρύση πουθενά;
here?
ipárhi vrísi poothená?

I want to hire a sailing boat Θέλω νά νοικιάσω ἱστιόπλοιο
(canoe, rowing boat, (κανώ, βάρκα, βενζινάκατο).
motor boat).
thélo ná nikiáso istióplio (kanó, várka, venzinákato)

We want to go fishing. Θέλουμε νά πᾶμε γιά ψάρεμα.
théloome ná páme yá psárema

Is there any shade on the beach?	Ὑπάρχει καθόλου σκιά στήν ἀμμουδιά;
	ipárhi kathóloo skyá stín amoothyá?
Is it deep here?	Εἶναι βαθειά ἐδῶ;
	íne vathyá ethó?
You will be out of your depth.	Δέν θά πατώνεις.
	thén thá patónis
Can I dive here?	Μπορῶ νά βουτήξω ἐδῶ;
	boró ná vootíkso ethó?
Yes, it's very deep. No, there are too many rocks.	Ναί, εἶναι πολύ βαθειά. Ὄχι ἔχει βράχια.
	né, íne polí vathyá. óhi, éhi vráhya
I cannot swim very well.	Δέν κολυμπάω καλά.
	thén kolimbáo kalá
Be careful, there is a strong current.	Πρόσεχε, ἔχει δυνατό ρεῦμα.
	prósehe, éhi thinató révma
Bathing prohibited.	Ἀπαγορεύται τό κολύμπι.
	apaghorévete tó kolími
Is the water cold?	Εἶναι τό νερό κρῦο;
	íne tó neró krío?
No, it's lovely.	Ὄχι, εἶναι θαῦμα.
	óhi, íne thávma
The rocks are covered with sea-urchins.	Τά βράχια εἶναι γεμάτα ἀχινούς.
	tá vráhya íne yemáta ahinoós
Are there many fish here?	Ὑπάρχουν ψάρια ἐδῶ;
	ipárhoon psária ethó?
Where is the best place for fish?	Ποιό εἶναι τό καλύτερο μέρος γιά ψάρεμα;
	pyó íne tó kalítero méros yá psárema?

SPORTS, GAMES AND ENTERTAINMENTS

VOCABULARY

athletics, ὁ ἀθλητισμός (ó athlitizmós)
athletics meetings, οἱ ἀθλητικές συναντήσεις, (μάτς) (i athlitikes sinandisis, match)
  high jump, τό ἅλμα εἰς ὕψος (tó álma ís ípsos)
  long jump, τό ἅλμα εἰς μῆκος (tó álma ís míkos)
  relay race, ἡ σκυταλοδρομία (i skitalothromía)
  hurdles, ὁ δρόμος μετ'ἐμποδίων (ó thrómos metembothíon)
  javelin, τό ἀκόντιον (tó akóndion)
  shot, ἡ σφαιροβολία (í sferovolía)
football, τό ποδόσφαιρο (tó pothósfero—also called "football")
  team, ἡ ὁμάδα (í omatha)
  goal, τό γκόλ (tó gól)
  ball, ἡ μπάλλα (í bála)
  referee, ὁ διαίτητής (ó thietitís)
game, race, match, ὁ ἀγώνας, ὁ ἀγώνας δρόμου, τό μάτς (ó aghónas, ó aghónas thrómoo, tó mátch)
horse racing, οἱ ἱπποδρομίες (í ipothromíes)
  bet, τό στοίχημα (tó stíhima)
  favourite, τό φαβορί (tó favorí)
  horse, τό ἄλογο (tó álogho)
  jockey, ὁ τζόκεϋ (ó tzókey)
  racecourse, τό ἱπποδρόμιο (tó ipothrómio)
  tote, τό πολλαπλοῦν (tó polaploón)
  winning-post, τό τέρμα (tó térma)
play, to, παίζω (pézo)
player, ὁ παίκτης (ó péktis)
opponent, ὁ ἀντίπαλος (ó andípalos)
score, τό σκόρ (tó skór)
ski-ing, σκί (skí)
  ski, to σκί (skí)
  skis, τά σκί (tá skí)
  ski-lift, ὁ ἀναβατήρας (ó anavatíras)
  ski-jump, τό ἅλμα (tó álma)
  ski run, ἡ πίστα (í písta)
  water-ski-ing, τό θαλάσσιο σκί (tó thalásio skí)
swimming, τό κολύμπι (tó kolímbi)
  dive, to, βουτάω (vootáo)
  swim, to, κολυμπάω (kolimbáo)
  swimming pool, ἡ πισίνα (í pisína)
  underwater swimming, τό ὑποβρύχιο κολύμπι (tó ipovríhio kolímbi)

tennis, τό τέννις (tó ténis) (*comparatively few people play tennis in Greece, and those who do all use the English terms*)
sports ground, football pitch, τό γήπεδον (to yípethon)

GAMES

backgammon, τό τάβλι (tó távli)
billiards, τό μπιλλιάρδο (tó bilyártho)
billiard table, τό τραπέζι τοῦ μπιλλιάρδου (tó trapézi toó bilyárthoo)
billiard cue, ἡ στέκα (í stéka)
bridge, τό μπρίτζ (tó brítz) (*if you play bridge with Greeks, you will find English or French terms generally understood*)
  ace, ὁ ἄσος (ó ásos)
  cards (playing), τά χαρτιά (tá hartyá)
  clubs, τά σπαθιά (tá spathyá)
  diamonds, τά καρρά (tá kará)
  hearts, οἱ κοῦπες (í koópes)
  king, ὁ ρήγας (ó ríghas)
  knave, ὁ βαλές (ὁ φάντης) (ó valés, ó fándis)
  pack (of cards), ἡ τράπουλα (í trápoola)
  queen, ἡ ντάμα (í dáma)
  spades, τά μπαστούνια (tá bastoónya)
  stake, ὁ πόντος (ó póndos)
  trick, ἡ χαρτωσιά (í hartosyá)
  trump, τό ἀτοῦ (tó atoó)
chess, τό σκάκι (tó skáki)
  bishop, ὁ ἐπίσκοπος (ó epískopos)
  board, ἡ σκακιέρα (í skakyéra)
  castling, τό ροκέ (tó roké)
  check, τό τσέκ (tó tsék)
  king, ὁ βασιληᾶς (ó vasilyás)
  knight, τό ἄλογο (tó álogho)
  mate, τό μάτ (tó mát)
  pawn, τό πιόνι (tó pyóni)
  queen, ἡ βασίλισσα (í vasílisa)
  rook, ὁ πῦργος (ó pírghos)
dice, τά ζάρια (tá zária)
dominoes, τό ντόμινο (tó dómino)
draughts, ἡ ντάμα (í dáma)
table-tennis, τό πίγκ-πόνγκ (tó píng-póng)

ENTERTAINMENT

ball, ὁ χορός (ó horós)
band, ἡ μπάντα (í bánda)
box (theatre), τό θεωρεῖο (θεάτρου) (tó theorío) (théatroo)
box-office, τό ταμεῖο (tó tamío)
casino, τό καζίνο (tó kazíno)
cinema, ὁ κινηματογράφος (τό σινεμά) (ó kinimatoghráfos, to sinemá)
cloakroom, τό βεστιάριο (tó vestiário)

cloakroom ticket, ὁ ἀριθμός βεστιαρίου (ό arithmos vestiaríoo)
comedy, ἡ κωμωδία (í komothía)
concert, ἡ συναυλία (í sinavlía)
concert-hall, ἡ αἴθουσα (í éthoosa)
dance, ὁ χορός (ó horós)
dance, to, χορεύω (horévo)
dancer, ὁ χορευτής, ἡ χορεύτρια (ό horeftís, í horéftia)
dress-circle, gallery, τό θεωρεῖο, ὁ ἐξώστης (tó theorío, ó eksóstis)
entertainment, ἡ διασκέδασις (í thiaskéthasis)
fancy-dress ball, ὁ χορός μεταμφιεσμένων (ό horós metamfiezménon)
festival, τό φεστιβάλ (tó festivál)
film, τό φίλμ (tó fílm)
folk dance, ὁ λαϊκός χορός (ó la-ikós horós)
interval, τό διάλειμμα (tó thiálima)
news cinema, ὁ κινηματόγραφος ἐπικαίρων (ό kinimatóghrafos epikéron)
night-club, τό νυκτερινό κέντρο (tó nikterinó kéndro)
opera, ἡ ὄπερα (í ópera)
orchestra, ἡ ὀρχήστρα (í orhístra)
pit, ἡ πλατεῖα (í platía)
play, τό θεατρικό ἔργο (tó theatrikó érgho)
revue, ἡ ἐπιθεώρηση (í epitheórisi)
seat, τό κάθισμα (tó káthizma)
show, τό θέαμα (tó théama)
stage, ἡ σκηνή (í skiní)
stalls, ἡ πλατεῖα (í platía)
theatre, τό θέατρο (tó théatro)
tragedy, ἡ τραγωδία (í traghothía)
usherette, ἡ ταξιθέτρια (í taksithétria)

In summer most of the indoor theatres and cinemas in Athens are closed, but many open-air ones flourish. Ancient drama is presented regularly at Epidauros and at the Roman theatre of Herodus Atticus, which is also used for orchestral concerts and performances by companies from abroad as part of the annual Athens Festival. Open-air theatres present revues, straight plays, Greek classics, Shakespeare and so on. Open-air cinemas appear in hundreds every summer, and are cheap and enjoyable.

Ubiquitous too is the "kéndron" κέντρον, or "centre", which may be anything from a sophisticated and expensive night-club to a bar with a juke-box.

Indoor cinemas have two prices, dearer downstairs and cheaper upstairs. At all cinemas and theatres it is customary to tip the usherette about one drachma for showing you to your seat.

Do you play tennis?   Παίζετε τέννις;
pézete ténnis?

Can we play tennis any-   Μπορούμε νά παίξουμε που-
where here?   θενά τέννις;
boroóme ná péksoome poothená ténnis?

What is the score?   Τί εῖναι τό σκόρ;

tí íne tó skór?

I want to go swimming.   Θέλω νά πάω νά κολυμπήσω.

thélo ná páo ná kolimbíso

Can I hire a bathing costume   Μπορῶ νά νοικιάσω μαγιό
(towel)?   (πετσέτα);

boró ná nikiáso mayó (petséta)?

We should like to ski (water-   Θέλω νά κάνω σκί (θαλάσσιο
ski).   σκί).

thélo ná káno skí (thalásio ski)

Can we hire the necessary   Μπορούμε νά νοικιάσουμε τά
equipment (boots, skis,   ἀπαραίτητα (ἀρβύλες, σκί,
sticks), here?   μπαστούνια) ἐδῶ;

boroóme ná nikiásoome tá aparétita (arvíles, skí, bastoónia) ethó?

It is terribly cold (hot). I am   Κάνει φοβερό κρῦο (ζέστη).
frozen (very hot).   Πάγωσα (ἔσκασα).

kámi foveró krío (zésti). pághosa (éskasa)

Can you recommend a ski-   Μπορεῖτε νά μοῦ συστήσετε
ing centre?   ποῦ νά κάνω σκί;

boríte ná moó sistísete poó ná káno skí?

How do we get there?   Πῶς μπορούμε νά πᾶμε;

pós boroóme ná páme

Are the runs long (difficult)?   Εῖναι μεγάλες οἱ πίστες (δύσ-

κολες);

íne megháles í pístes (thískoles)?

There has been a heavy   Ἔχει πέσει πολύ χιόνι.
snowfall.

éhi pési polí hyóni

Are you going to the races?   Θά πᾶτε στίς ἱπποδρομίες;

thá páte stís ippothromíes?

Which is the favourite?   Ποιό εῖναι τό φαβορί;

pyó íne tó favorí?

Have you won anything?   Κέρδισες τίποτα;

kérthises típota?

A hundred drachmas to win   Ἑκατό δραχμές γκανιάν στό . . .
on . . .

ekató thrahmés ganyán stó . . .

Fifty drachmas a place on... Πενῆντα δραχμές πλασέ στό...
penínda thrahmés plasé stó...

A hundred and fifty each way on... Ἑκατό πενῆντα σύνθετο...
ekató penínda sínθeto stó...

Would you care for a game of...? Παίζουμε ἕνα παιγνίδι...;
pézoome éna peghníθi...?

Would you like to dance? Θέλετε νά χορέψουμε;
θélete ná horépsoome?

I don't know how to dance this. Δέν ξέρω νά χορεύω αὐτό.
θén kséro ná horévo aftó

Do you know what is on at the cinema (theatre)? Ξέρετε τί παίζουν τά σινεμά (τό θέατρο);
ksérete tí pézoon tá sinemá (tó θéatro)?

Who is playing in it? Ποιός παίζει;
pyós pézi?

Should we book seats? Πρέπει νά κλείσουμε θέσεις;
prépi ná klísoome θésis?

Would you like to come? Θέλετε ναρθῆτε;
θélete narθíte?

Have you any seats at 25 drachmas for Saturday evening (afternoon)? Ἔχετε θέσεις τῶν 25 δραχμῶν γιά Σάββατο βράδυ (ἀπόγευμα);
éhete θésis tón íkosi pénde thrahmón yá sávato vráθi (apóyevma)

Show me where they are on the plan. Δεῖξτε μου ποῦ εἶναι στό σχεδιάγραμμα.
θíkstemoo poó íne stó skheθyághrama

Two downstairs (balcony), please. Δύο πλατεῖα (ἐξώστη) παρακαλῶ.
θío platía (eksósti) parakaló

It was a very good film (play). Ἦταν πολύ ὡραῖο ἔργο.
ítan polí oréo érgho

Enjoy yourselves! Καλή διασκέδαση!
kalí θiaskéθasi!

HIKING, CAMPING AND WEATHER

There are one or two authorized camping-grounds near Athens, but in general camping is not an organized activity in Greece.   There are one or two hostels in large towns, such as the Y.M.C.A. and Y.W.C.A. and students may find dormitory accommodation at the University Club in Athens. The Greek Mountaineering Club maintains huts on a number of mountains, which may be used by non-members for a small charge.

air mattress, ἀερόστρωμα (aeróstroma)
boots, οἱ ἀρβῦλες (í arvíles)
blanket, ἡ κουβέρτα (í koovérta)
bottle opener, τό κλειδί (tó klithí)
bridge, ἡ γέφυρα (í yéfira)
bucket, ὁ κουβᾶς (ó koovás)
camp, ἡ κατασκήνωση (í kataskínosi)
camping equipment, τό κατασκηνωτικό ὑλικό (tó kataskinotikó ilikó)
camping site, ἡ τοποθεσία κατασκηνώσεως (í topothesía kataskinóseos)
candle, τό κερί (tó kerí)
climbing, ἡ ἀναρρίχηση (í anaríhisi)
cold, τό κρύο (tó krío)
cooking utensils, τά μαγειρικά σκεύη (tá mayiriká skévi)
corkscrew, τό τιρμπουσόν (tó tirboosón)
country, ἡ ἐξοχή (í eksohí)
dawn, ἡ αὐγή (í avyí)
drinking water, τό πόσιμο νερό (tó pósimo neró)
farm, ἡ φάρμα, τό ἀγρόκτημα (í fárma, tó aghróktima)
farmer, ὁ ἀγροκτηματίας (ó aghroktimatías)
field, ὁ ἀγρός (ó aghrós)
forest, τό δάσος (tó thásos)
frying-pan, τό τηγάνι (tó tigháni)
groundsheet, ὁ μουσαμᾶς (ó moosamás)
haversack, τό σακίδιο (tó sakíthyo)
heat, ἡ ζέστη (í zésti)
hitch-hike, to, κάνω ὠτοστόπ (káno ótostop)
hill, ὁ λόφος (ó lófos)
hot, ζεστό (zestó)
hut, mountain refuge, ἡ καλύβα, τό καταφύγιο (í kalíva, tó katafíyo)
ice, ὁ πάγος (ó pághos)
lake, ἡ λίμνη (í límni)
lane, ὁ χωματόδρομος (ó homatóthromos)
lightning, ἡ ἀστραπή (í astrapí)
log, ὁ κορμός (ó kormós)
map, ὁ χάρτης (ó hártis)
matches, τά σπίρτα (tá spírta)

mess-tin, ἡ καραβάνα (i karaváนa)
methylated spirit, τό οίνόπνευμα (tó inópnevma)
mist, ἡ ὁμίχλη (í omíhli)
mosquito-net, ἡ κουνουπιέρα (í koonoopyéra)
moss, τό μοῦσκλο, ἡ χλόη (tó moósklo, i hlóy)
mountain, τό βουνό (tó voonó)
mountain pass, τό πέρασμα (tó pérazma)
paraffin, τό πετρέλαιο καθαρό (tó petréleo katharó)
path, τό μονοπάτι (tó monopáti)
penknife, ὁ σουγιᾶς (ó sooyás)
picnic, τό πίκ-νίκ (tó píkník)
pole, ὁ πάσσαλος (ó pásalos)
rain, ἡ βροχή (í vrohí)
ravine, ὁ γκρεμός (ó gremós)
river, τό ποτάμι (tó potámi)
road, ὁ δρόμος (ó **thr**ómos)
rope, τό σχοινί (tó skhiní)
rubbish, refuse, τά σκουπίδια, (tá skoopí**th**ya)
refuse bin, ὁ σκουπιδοτενεκές (ó skoopi**th**otenckés)
rucksack, τό σακκίδιο (tó sakí**th**yo)
sandwich, τό σάντουϊτς (tó sándwich)
saucepan, ὁ τέντζερης (ó téndzeris)
shepherd, ὁ βοσκός (ó voskós)
shower (*of rain*), ἡ μπόρα (í bóra)
sleeping-bag, ὁ σάκκος ὕπνου (ó sákos ípnoo)
snow, τό χιόνι (to hyóni)
storm, ἡ καταιγίδα (í kateyí**th**a)
stove (*paraffin*), ἡ γκαζιέρα (í gazyéra)
stream, τό ρυάκι (tó ryáki)
summit, ἡ κορυφή (í korifí)
tent, τό ἀντίσκηνο (tó andískino)
tent peg, τό καρφί (tó karfí)
tent pole, ὁ πάσαλος (ó pásalos)
tent, to pitch, στήνω τό ἀντίσκοινο (stíno tó andískino)
thermos, τό θερμός (tó thermós)
thunder, ἡ βροντή (í vrondí)
tin-opener, ὁ κονσερβανοίχτης (ó konservaníhtis)
torch, ὁ φακός (ó fakós)
valley, ἡ κοιλάδα (í kilá**th**a)
village, τό χωριό (tó horyó)
walk, ὁ περίπατος (ó perípatos)
waterfall, ὁ καταράκτης (ó kataráktis)
waterproof, τό ἀδιάβροχο (tó a**th**yávroho)
weather, ὁ καιρός (ó kerós)
good, bad, weather, ὁ καλός, κακός, καιρός (ó kalós, kakós, kerós)
wind, ὁ ἄνεμος (ó ánemos)
wood, τό δάσος (tó **th**ásos)
Y.M.C.A., Χ.Α.Ν. (hán)
Y.W.C.A., Χ.Ε.Ν. (hén)

Where does this road lead?   Ποῦ πηγαίνει αὐτός ὁ δρόμος;
poó piyéni aftós ó thrómos?

How long does it take to...?   Πόση ὥρα κάνει γιά...;
pósi óra káni yá...?

The next town (village) is   Εἶναι πέντε χιλιόμετρα ἀπ'ἐδῶ
five kms. from here.   ὡς τήν ἐπόμενη πόλι (χωριό).
íne pénde hilyómetra ap ethó ós tín epómeni póli (horyó)

What is the name of this   Πῶς λέγεται αὐτό τό μέρος;
place?
pós léyete aftó tó méros?

Where is the square?   Ποῦ εἶναι ἡ πλατεῖα;
poó íne í platía?

Can you recommend a cheap   Μπορεῖτε νά μοῦ συστήσετε
restaurant?   ἕνα φθηνό ἐστιατόριο;
boríte ná moó sistísete éna fthinó estiatório?

It is too dear. Have you any-   Εἶναι πολύ ἀκριβό.   Ἔχετε
thing cheaper?   τίποτα φθηνότερο;
íne polí akrivó.   éhete típota fthinótero?

I should like to wash.   Θά ἤθελα νά πλυθῶ.
thá íthela ná plithó

Is this drinking water?   Εἶναι τό νερό αὐτό πόσιμο;
íne tó neró aftó pósimo?

Is there a Y.M.C.A. near   Ὑπάρχει κανένας ξενώνας τῆς
here?   Χ.Α.Ν ἐδῶ κοντά;
ipárhi kanénas ksenónas tís HAN ethó kondá?

It is half-way up (down).   Εἶναι στά μισά τοῦ δρόμου.
íne stá misá toó thrómoo

Can we cut across country?   Μπορούμε νά κόψουμε δρόμο;
boroóme ná kópsoome thrómo?

We want to keep to the main   Θέλομε νά μείνωμε στόν κεντρι-
road.   κό δρόμο.
thélome ná mínome stón kentrikó thrómo

We are lost.   Χαθήκαμε.
hathíkame

We are looking for some-   Ζητᾶμε μέρος νά κατασκηνώσ-
where to camp.   ωμε.
zitáme méros ná kataskinósome

We are looking for the camping-site.	Ζητᾶμε τοποθεσία κατασκηνώσεως. zitáme topothesía kataskinóseos
Where can I buy paraffin (methylated spirit)?	Ποῦ μπορῶ ν'ἀγοράσω πετρέλαιο (οἰνόπνευμα); poó boró naghoráso petréleo (inópnevma)?
May we light a fire ?	Μποροῦμε ν'ἀνάψωμε φωτιά; boroóme nanápsome fotyá?
It is very dangerous. The grass is very dry.	Εἶναι πολύ ἐπικίνδυνο. Τό χορτάρι εἶναι πολύ ξερό. íne polí epikínthino. tó hortári íne polí kseró
Beware of the dog.	Προσοχή στό σκύλο. prosohí stó skílo
Turn off the tap.	Κλεῖστε τή βρύση. klíste tí vrísi
Rubbish bin.	Ὁ σκουπιδοντενεκές. o skoopithodenekés
It is very hot (cold).	Κάνει ζέστη (κρῦο). káni zésti (krío)
There is a lot of dust.	Ἔχει πολύ σκόνη. éhi polí skóni
There are too many mosquitoes.	Ἔχει πολλά κουνούπια. éhi polá koonoópya
Is the ascent difficult?	Εἶναι δύσκολη ἡ ἀνάβαση; íne thískoli í anávasi?
It takes five hours.	Εἶναι πέντε ὧρες. íne pénde óres
It is very rocky.	Εἶναι βραχῶδες. íne vrahóthes
It is all thorny scrub.	Εἶναι γεμάτο ἀγκάθια. íne yemáto angkáthya
You will need a guide.	Θά χρειαστῆτε ὁδηγό. thá hriastíte othighó
The path is blocked by snow.	Τό μονοπάτι ἔκλεισε μέ τό χιόνι. tó monopáti éklise mé tó hyóni

It is lovely (terrible) weather.	Εἶναι ὡραῖος (ἀπαίσιος) καιρός.
	íne oréos (apésyos) kerós
It looks like rain.	Φαίνεται πώς θά βρέξη.
	fénete pós thá vréksi
It is only a shower.	Μπόρα εἶναι μόνο.
	bóra íne móno
It is going to be windy.	Θά πιάσει ἀέρας.
	thá pyási aéras
I didn't understand the weather forecast. Will you explain it?	Δέν κατάλαβα τό μετεωρολο- γικό δελτίο. Μοῦ τό ἐξηγῆτε;
	thén katálava tó meteoroloyikó theltío. moó tó eksiyíte?

SHOPPING

SHOPKEEPERS AND SHOPS

The shop is indicated by an apostrophe "s" to distinguish it from the shop-keeper. Where two Greek translations are given, the first is the popular or spoken term, and the second the official or written term.

baker, ὁ φούρναρης (ó foórnaris)
baker's, τό ἀρτοποιεῖον (tó artopiíon)
bank, ἡ τράπεζα (í trápeza)
barber's, τό κουρεῖον (tó kooríon)
bookshop, τό βιβλιοπωλεῖον (tó vivliopolíon)
butcher, ὁ χασάπης (ó hasápis)
butcher's, τό κρεοπωλεῖον (tó kreopolíon)
cake-shop, τό ζαχαροπλαστεῖον (tó zaharoplastíon)
chemist's, τό φαρμακεῖον (tó farmakíon)
cleaner's and dyer's, τό στεγνοκαθαριστήριο (tó steghnoka-
    tharistírio)
dairy, τό γαλακτοπωλεῖον (tó ghalaktopolíon)
draper's, τό ἐμπορικόν (tó emborikón)
dressmaker, ἡ μοδίστρα (í mothístra)
electrical goods, ἠλεκτρικά εἴδη (ílektriká íthi)
electrician, ὁ ἠλεκτρολόγος (ó ilektróloghos)
fishmonger, ὁ ψαρᾶς (ó psarás)
fishmonger's, τό ἰχθυοπωλεῖον (tó ihthyopolíon)
florist's, τό ἀνθοπωλεῖον (tó anthopolíon)
furrier's, τό γουνάδικο (tó ghoonáthiko)
greengrocer, ὁ μανάβης (ó manávis)
greengrocer's, τό μανάβικο, τό ὀπωροπωλεῖον (tó manáviko, tó
    oporopolíon)

grocer's, τό μπακάλικο, τό παντοπωλεῖον (tó bakáliko, to pandopolíon)
grocer, ὁ μπακάλης (ó bakális)
haberdashery, τά ψιλικά (tá psiliká)
hairdresser (*for women*), ὁ κομμωτής (ó komotís)
hairdresser's, τό κομμωτήριον (tó komotírion)
ironmonger's, ὑδραυλικά (ithravliká)
jeweller's, τό κοσμηματοπωλεῖον (tó kosmimatopolíon)
kiosk, τό περίπτερο (tó períptero)
market, ἡ ἀγορά (í aghorá)
milkman, ὁ γαλατᾶς (ó ghalatás)
perfumery, τό ἀρωματοπωλεῖον (tó aromatopolíon)
photographic shop, τό φωτογραφεῖον (tó fotoghrafíon)
shoemaker (*repairs*), ὁ τσαγκάρης (ó tsangkáris)
shoe-shop, τό ὑποδηματοποιεῖον (tó ipothimatopíon)
shop, τό μαγαζί (tó maghazí)
stationer, τό χαρτοπωλεῖον (tó hartopolíon)
tailor, ὁ ράφτης (ó ráftis)
travel-agent, τό πρακτορεῖον ταξιδίων (tó praktoríon taksithíon)

Kiosks. Every hundred yards or so along main streets there is a kiosk set up on the pavement. This is where you buy stamps, cigarettes, news-papers, chocolate, pencils, razor-blades and so on. In the centre of Athens they sell foreign papers and books too, and some stay open till very late at night.

POST OFFICE AND TELEPHONE

Postage stamps in Greece may be bought from certain of the pavement kiosks as well as from the Post Office. Telegrams are not taken at Post Offices but at the offices of OTE, the State Telecommunications Organization. Telephone call-boxes are not all that common, but local calls may always be made from a kiosk or shop. Call-boxes do not accept coins, but metal counters called kérmata, which may be bought at kiosks near the box.

VOCABULARY

cable(gram), τό τηλεγράφημα (tó tileghráfima)
call (*telephone*), τό τηλεφώνημα (tó tilefónima)
call-box, ὁ τηλεφωνικός θάλαμος (ó tilefonikós thálamos)
counter, ὁ πάγκος (ó pángkos)
delivery, ἡ παραλαβή (í paralaví)
directory (*telephone*), ὁ τηλεφωνικός κατάλογος (ó tilefonikós katáloghos)
letter, τό γράμμα (to ghráma)
parcel, τό δέμα (to théma)
post office, τό ταχυδρομεῖο (to tahithromío)
postal order, ἡ ταχυδρομική ἐπιταγή (i tahithromikí epitayí)
postcard, ἡ κάρτα (i kárta)
money order, ἡ ταχυδρομική ἐπιταγή (i tahithromikí epitayí)

postman, ὁ ταχυδρόμος (ó tahi**thr**ómos)
number, ὁ ἀριθμός (ó arithmós)
register, to, συστήνω (sistíno)
reply paid, ἀπάντησις πληρωμένη (apándisis pliroméni)
stamp, τό γραμματόσημο (tó ghramatósimo)
telegram, τό τηλεγράφημα (tó tileghráfima)
telegraph office, τό τηλεγραφεῖο (tó tileghrafío)
telephone, τό τηλέφωνο (tó tiléfono)

ΕΔΩ ΤΗΛΕΦΩΝΕΙΤΕ, **Telephone Here** (eth**ó** tilefoníte)
ΤΗΛΕΦΩΝΟ ΔΙΑ ΤΟ ΚΟΙΝΟ, **Public Telephone** (tiléfono thiá tó kinó)

Is there a post office near here?
Ὑπάρχει ταχυδρομεῖο ἐδῶ κοντά;
ipárhi tahi**thr**omío ethó kondá?

Do you sell stamps?
Πουλᾶτε γραμματόσημα;
pooláte ghramatósima?

Do you know how much it is for England?
Ξέρετε πόσο εἶναι γιά τήν Ἀγγλία;
ksérete póso íne yá tín anglía?

Where is it for?
Γιά ποῦ εἶναι;
yá poó íne?

I want to send this parcel.
Θέλω νά στείλω αὐτό τό δέμα.
thélo ná stílo aftó tó **thé**ma

I want to register this letter.
Θέλω νά στείλω αὐτό τό γράμμα συστημένο.
thélo ná stílo aftó tó ghráma sistiméno

Give me the receipt, please.
Δῶστε μου τήν ἀπόδειξη, παρακαλῶ.
thóstemoo tín apó**th**iksi, parakaló

Where is the Poste Restante?
Ποῦ εἶναι τό Πόστ Ρεστάντ;
poó íne tó póst restánt?

Are there any letters for me?
Ἔχει γράμματα γιά μένα;
éhi ghrámata yá ména?

Your passport, please.
Τό διαβατήριό σας, παρακαλῶ.
tó **th**iávatiriósas, parakaló

May I make a phone call, please?
Μπορῶ νά κάνω ἕνα τηλεφώνημα, παρακαλῶ;
boró ná káno éna tilefónima, parakaló?

Give me a telephone counter, please.   Μοῦ δίνετε ἕνα κέρμα τηλεφώνου, παρακαλῶ.

moó thínete éna kérma tilefónoo, parakaló

How much is it?   Πόσο κάνει;

póso káni?

Would you get me this number, please?   Μοῦ παίρνετε αὐτό τόν ἀριθμό, παρακαλῶ;

moó pérnete aftó tón arithmó, parakaló?

I can't hear you.   Δέν ἀκούω.

thén akoó-o

Who is speaking?   Ποιός εἶναι ἐκεῖ;

pyós íne ekí?

Would you give me Mr. . . . , please.   Μοῦ δίνετε τόν κύριο . . ., παρακαλῶ.

moó thínete τόν kírio . . ., parakaló

Mr. . . . himself speaking.   Ὁ ἴδιος.

o íthyos

Hold the line, please.   Περιμένετε στό ἀκουστικό σας, παρακαλῶ.

periménete stó akoostikósas, parakaló

I will call him (her).   Θά τόν (τήν) φωνάξω.

thá tón (tín) fonákso

Wrong number.   Λάθος.

láthos

What number do you want?   Τί ἀριθμό θέλετε;

tí arithmó thélete?

How much do I owe you for the call?   Πόσο κάνει τό τηλεφώνημα;

póso káni tó tilefónima?

CHEMIST AND HAIRDRESSER

VOCABULARY

antiseptic, τό ἀντισηπτικό (τό andisiptikó)
aspirin, ἡ ἀσπιρίνη (ί aspiríni)
bathsalts, τά ἀρωματικά ἅλατα (tá aromatiká álata)

brilliantine, ἡ μπριγιαντίνη (í briyandíni)
brush, ἡ βούρτσα (í voórtsa)
brush (*nail*), ἡ βούρτσα νυχιῶν (í voórtsa nihyón)
brush (*tooth*), ἡ ὀδοντόβουρτσα (í othondóvoortsa)
colour rinse, τό χρωμοσαμπουάν (tó hromosampooán)
comb, ἡ κτένα (í kténa)
cosmetics, τά καλλυντικά (tá kalindiká)
cotton-wool, τό βαμβάκι (tó vamváki)
cream (*cosmetic*) ἡ καλλυντική κρέμα (í kalindikí kréma)
cough sweets, οἱ καραμέλες τοῦ βῆχα (í karaméles toó víha)
dryer, τό σεσουάρ (to sesooár)
dye, to, βάφω (váfo)
dye, ἡ βαφή (í vafí)
gargle, ἡ γαργάρα (í gharghára)
hair, ἡ τρίχα (í tríha)
hair curler, τό μπικουτί (tó bikootí)
hair grip, τό τσιμπιδάκι (tó tsimbitháki)
hair lacquer, ἡ λάκα (í láka)
hair pins, ἡ φουρκέτα (í foorkéta)
laxative, τό καθαρτικό (tó kathartikó)
lipstick, τό κραγιόν (tó krayón)
lotion, ἡ λοσιόν (í losyón)
medicine, τό φάρμακο (tó fármako)
nail, τό νύχι (tó níhi)
nail file, ἡ λίμα νυχιῶν (í líma nihyón)
nail scissors, τό ψαλίδι νυχιῶν (tó psalíthi nihyón)
nail varnish, τό μανόν (tó manón)
ointment, ἡ ἀλοιφή (í alifí)
parting, ἡ χωρίστρα (í horístra)
perfume, τό ἄρωμα (tó ároma)
perfume, bottle of, τό μπουκαλάκι ἀρώματος (tó bookaláki arómatos)
prescription, ἡ συνταγή (í sindayí)
powder (*face*), ἡ πούδρα (í poóthra)
powder (*talcum*), τό τάλκ (tó tálk)
powder compact, ἡ πουδριέρα (í poodriéra)
powder puff, τό πομπόν (tó pombón)
razor blades, τά ξυραφάκια (tá ksirafákya)
rollers, τά ρολλά (tá rolá)
sanitary towels, οἱ πετσέτες ὑγείας (í petsétes iyías)
shampoo, τό σαμπουάν (tó sampooán)
shaving brush, τό πινέλο ξυρίσματος (tó pinélo ksirízmatos)
shaving cream, ἡ κρέμα ξυρίσματος (í kréma ksirízmatos)
shaving soap, τό σαπούνι ξυρίσματος (tó sapóoni ksirízmatos)
sleeping pill, τά ὑπνωτικά χάπια (tá ipnotiká hápya)
soap, τό σαπούνι (tó sapóoni)
sticking-plaster, ὁ λευκοπλάστης (ó lefkoplástis)
sunglasses, τά γυαλιά ἡλίου (tá yalyá ilíoo)
suntan cream, ἡ κρέμα ἡλίου (í kréma ilíoo)
toilet-paper, τό χαρτί τουαλέττας (tó hartí tooalétas)

toothpaste, ἡ ὀδοντόπαστα (í othondópasta)
wave, ἡ σκάλα (í skála)
wave (*permanent*), ἡ περμανάντ (í permanánt)
wave set, τό μιζαμπλί (tó mizamblí)

Can I make an appointment? Μπορῶ νά κλείσω ἕνα ραντεβοῦ;
boró ná klíso éna randevoó?

I want a shave. Θέλω ξύρισμα.
thélo ksírizma

Just a haircut. Μόνο κόψιμο.
móno kópsimo

I want my hair trimmed. Θέλω ἐλαφρό κόψιμο.
thélo elafró kópsimo

Don't cut it too short behind Μήν τά κόψετε κοντά πίσω
(in front). (μπρός).
mín tá kópsete kondá píso (brós)

I would like it short at the Τά θέλω κοντά πίσω καί στά
back and sides. πλάγια.
tá thélo kondá píso ké stá pláya

Don't put anything on my Νά μή βάλετε τίποτα στά
hair. μαλλιά μου.
ná mí válete típota stá malyámoo

I want my nails manicured. Θέλω μανικιούρ.
thélo manikyoór

I want a shampoo and set. Θέλω σαμπουάν καί μιζαμπλί.
thélo sampooán ké mizamblí

I want a perm (colour rinse). Θέλω περμανάντ (χρωμο-σαμ-
πουάν).
thélo permanánt (hrómo-sampooán)

Please set my hair with Νά μοῦ τυλίξετε τά μαλλιά μου
(without) rollers. μέ (χωρίς) ρολλά.
ná moo tilíksete tá malyámoo mé (horís) rolá

The water is too hot, you are Τό νερό εἶναι πολύ ζεστό, μέ
scalding me. κάψατε.
tó neró íne polí zestó, mé kápsate

The dryer is too hot; can you adjust it?
Τό σεσουάρ εῖναι πολύ- ζεστό. Μπορεῖτε νά τό ρυθμίσετε;
tó sesooár íne polí zestó.   boríte ná tó rithmísete?

My hair is dry.
Τά μαλλιά μου στέγνωσαν.
tá malyámoo stéghnosan

I would like some brilliantine (lacquer).
Θέλω λίγη μπριγιαντίνη (λάκα).
thélo líyi briyandíni (láka)

Thank you. That is very nice.
Εὐχαριστῶ. Εῖναι πολύ ὡραῖα.
efharistó.   íne polí oréa

Can you make up this prescription, please?
Μοῦ φτιάχνετε αὐτή τή συνταγή, παρακαλῶ;
moó ftiáhnete aftí tí sindayí, parakaló?

It is an English prescription.
Εῖναι ἀγγλική συνταγή.
íne anglikí sindayí

Can you give me something for diarrhoea (headache, indigestion, sea-sickness)?
Ἔχετε τίποτα γιά διάρροια (πονοκέφαλο, δυσπεψία, ναυτία);
éhete típota yá thiária (ponokéfalo, thispepsía, naftia)?

I have been burnt by the sun.
Ἔχω ἔγκαυμα ἀπό τόν ἥλιο.
ého éngkavma apó tón ílyo

My skin is smarting; have you anything to soothe it?
Τό δέρμα μου τσούζει, ἔχετε τίποτα νά μέ ἀνακουφίσει;
tó thérmamoo tsoózi, éhete típota ná mé anakoofísi?

How much must I take?
Πόσο νά παίρνω;
póso ná pérno?

How often must I take it?
Κάθε πότε νά τό παίρνω;
káthe póte ná tó pérno?

One teaspoonful (tablespoonful) in a glass of water.
Ἕνα κουταλάκι τοῦ τσαγιοῦ (φαγητοῦ) σ᾽ἕνα ποτῆρι νερό.
éna kootaláki toó tsayoó (fayitoó) séna potíri neró

Take ... three times a day (every four hours) before (after) meals.
Παίρνετε ... τρεῖς φορές τή μέρα (κάθε τέσσερες ὧρες) πρό (μετά) φαγητοῦ.
pérnete ... trís forés tí méra (káthe téseris óres) pró (metá) fayitoó

PHOTOGRAPHY

VOCABULARY

camera, ἡ φωτογραφικὴ μηχανή (í fotoghrafikí mihaní)
case, ἡ θήκη (í thíki)
cine-camera, ἡ κινηματογραφικὴ μηχανή (í kinimatoghrafikí mihaní)
develop, to, ἐμφανίζω (emfanízo)
enlarge, to, μεγενθύνω (meyenthíno)
enlargement, ἡ μεγένθυσις (í meyénthisis)
film, τὸ φίλμ (tó fílm)
film (colour), τὸ ἔγχρωμο φίλμ (tó énghromo fílm)
film winder, τὸ κλειδὶ περιτυλίξεως (tó klithí peritilíkseos)
filter, τὸ φίλτρο (tó fíltro)
flash bulb, τὸ φλάς (tó flás)
glossy, γυαλιστερό (yalisteró)
lens, ὁ φακός (ó fakós)
lens-hood, τὸ παρασολέ (tó parasolé)
light meter, τὸ φωτόμετρο (tó fotómetro)
matt, μάτ (mát)
negative, ἀρνητικό (tó arnitikó)
print, ἡ ἐκτύπωση (í ektíposi)
print, to, ἐκτυπώνω (ektipóno)
range-finder, τὸ τηλέμετρο (tó tilémetro)
shutter, τὸ κλεῖστρο (tó klístro)
size, τὸ μέγεθος (tó méyethos)
spool, ἡ μπομπίνα (í bobína)
tripod, τὸ τρίποδο (tó trípotho)
view-finder, τὸ σκόπευτρο (tó skópeftro)

Have you any fast (fine Ἔχετε γρήγορο (λεπτόκοκκο,
grain, colour) film? ἔγχρωμο) φίλμ;
       éhete ghríghoro (leptókoko, énghromo) fílm?

What size do you want? Τί μέγεθος θέλετε;
       tí méyethos thélete?

Have you got the camera Ἔχετε μαζί σας τὴ φωτογρα-
with you? φική μηχανή;
       éhete mazísas tí fotoghrafikí mihaní?

I want miniature (one- Θέλω φίλμ τριανταπέντε χιλι-
twenty) film. οστόν (ἑκατόν εἴκοσι).
       thélo fílm triánda pénde hilyostón (ekatón íkosi)

I want a reversal (negative) colour film. Θέλω ἕνα ἀντιστρεφόμενο (ἀρνητικό) ἔγχρωμο φίλμ.
thélo éna andistrefómeno (arnitikó) énghromo film

The price includes developing. Στήν τιμή περιλαμβάνεται καί ἡ ἐμφάνιση.
stín timí perilamvánete ké í emfánisi

Will you develop this film, please. Μπορεῖτε νά ἐμφανίσετε αὐτό τό φίλμ, παρακαλῶ;
boríte ná emfanísete aftó tó film, parakaló?

I want two prints of each. Θέλω δύο ἀντίτυπα τό καθένα.
thélo thío andítipa tó kathéna

When will they be ready? Πότε θἆναι ἕτοιμα;
póte tháne étima?

Will you enlarge this, please. Μπορεῖτε νά μεγενθύνετε αὐτό, παρακαλῶ;
boríte ná meyenthínete aftó, parakaló?

They are under-exposed (over-exposed). Εἶναι ὑποφωτισμένα (ὑπερφωτισμένα).
íne ipofotizména (iperfotizména)

. . . doesn't work. . . . δέν δουλεύει.
. . . thén thoolévi

The film is jammed. Τό φίλμ εἶναι μπλεγμένο.
tó film íne bleghméno

The knob won't turn. Τό κουμπί δέν γυρνάει.
tó koombí thén yirnái

Can you repair spectacles? Διορθώνετε γυαλιά;
thiorthónete yalyá?

MISCELLANEOUS

VOCABULARY

bag, ἡ σακκούλα (í sakoóla)
battery, ἡ μπαταρία (í bataría)
book, τό βιβλίο (tó vivlío)
bracelet, τό βραχιόλι (tó vrahyóli)
braces, οἱ τιράντες (í tirándes)
brooch, ἡ καρφίτσα (í karfítsa)

bulb, ὁ γλόμπος (ó ghlómbos)
button, τό κουμπί (tó koombí)
card, ἡ κάρτα (í kárta)
card (*birthday*), ἡ κάρτα (γενεθλίων) (í kárta, yenethlíon)
card (*Christmas*), ἡ Χριστουγεννιάτικη κάρτα (í hristooyenyátiki
    kárta)
cardboard, τό χαρτόνι (tó hartóni)
cheap, φτηνό (ftinó)
cigar, τό ποῦρο (tó poóro)
cigarette (*filter-tipped*), τό τσιγάρο (φίλτρο) (tó tsigháro (fíltro)
collar stud, τό ξενόκουμπο κολλάρου (tó ksenókoombo kolároo)
cotton, ἡ κλωστή (í klostí)
cuff-links, τά μανικέτια (tá manikétya)
dark, σκοῦρο (skoóro)
dear, ἀκριβό (akrivó)
dictionary, τό λεξικό (tó leksikó)
disinfectant, τό ἀπολυμαντικό (tó apolimandikó)
doll, ἡ κοῦκλα (í koókla)
earrings, τά σκουλαρίκια (tá skoolaríkya)
elastic, τό λάστιχο (tó lástiho)
embroidery, τό κέντημα (tó kéndima)
envelope, ὁ φάκελλος (ó fákelos)
gloves, τά γάντια (tá ghándya)
gramophone record, ὁ δίσκος (ó thískos)
guide-book, ὁ ὁδηγός (ó othigós)
handbag, ἡ τσάντα (í tsánda)
hat, τό καπέλλο (to kapélo)
heavy, βαρύ (varí)
heel, τό τακούνι (tó takoóni)
ink, ἡ μελάνη (i meláni)
insecticide, τό ἐντομοκτόνο (tó endomoktóno)
invisible mending, τό ἀόρατο μαντάρισμα (tó aórato mandárizma)
label, ἡ ταμπέλα (í tabéla)
lace, ἡ ταντέλλα (í tandéla)
large, μεγάλο (meghálo)
light (*in colour*), ἀνοιχτό (anihtó)
light (*in weight*), ἐλαφρό (elafró)
lighter (*cigarette*), ὁ ἀναπτήρας (ó anaptíras)
lighter flint, ἡ τσακμακόπετρα (í tsakmakópetra)
lighter fuel, ἡ βενζίνη, ὁ ἀναπτήρας (í venzíni, ó anaptíras)
lighter (*gas*), ὁ ἀναπτήρας γκαζιοῦ (ó anaptíras gazyoó)
long, μακρύ (makrí)
magazine, τό περιοδικό (tó periothikó)
map, ὁ χάρτης (ó hártis)
matches, τά σπίρτα (tá spírta)
material, τό ὕφασμα (tó ífazma)
narrow, στενό (stenó)
necklace, τό κολλιέ (tó kolyé)
needle, ἡ βελόνα (í velóna)

newspaper, ἡ ἐφημερίδα (í efimerítha)
paper, τό χαρτί (tó hartí)
pen (*ball-point*), ἡ πέννα (í péna)
pen (*fountain*), τό στυλό (tó stiló)
pencil, τό μολύβι (tó molívi)
pipe, ἡ πίπα (í pípa)
pin, ἡ καρφίτσα (í karfítsa)
pin (*safety*), ἡ παραμάνα (í paramána)
plan, τό σχέδιο (tó skhéthyo)
purse, τό πορτοφόλι (tó portofóli)
raincoat, τό ἀδιάβροχο (tó athiávroho)
razor, ἡ ξυριστική μηχανή (í ksiristikí mihaní)
razor blades, τά ξυραφάκια (tá ksirafákya)
refill, τό ἀνταλλακτικό (tó andalaktikó)
ribbon, ἡ κορδέλα (í korthéla)
ring, τό δακτυλίδι (tó thaktilíthi)
sales, οἱ ἐκπτώσεις (í ekptósis)
sandals, τά πέδιλα (tá péthila)
scissors, τό ψαλίδι (tó psalíthi)
self-service, ἡ αὐτοεξυπηρέτησις (í aftoeksipirétisis)
shoes, τά παπούτσια (tá papoótsya)
shoe-laces, τά κορδόνια (tá korthónya)
shoe polish, τό βερνίκι (tó verníki)
shop, τό μαγαζί (tó maghazí)
shop assistant, ὁ ὑπάλληλος (ó ipálilos)
short, κοντό (kondó)
silk, τό μεταξωτό (tó metaksotó)
size, τό μέγεθος (tó méyethos)
small, μικρό (mikró)
soap, τό σαπούνι (tó sapoóni)
sole, ἡ σόλα (í sóla)
souvenir, τό ἐνθύμιο (tó enthímio)
spade, τό φτυάρι (tó ftyári)
spectacles, τά γυαλιά (tá yalyá)
stick, τό μπαστούνι (tó bastoóni)
strap, τό λουρί (tó loorí)
string, ὁ σπάγγος (ó spángos)
suitcase, ἡ βαλίτσα (í valítsa)
sun-hat, ἡ ψάθα (í psátha)
thick, χοντρό (hondró)
thimble, ἡ δακτυλήθρα (í thaktilíthra)
thin, λεπτό (leptó)
thread, ἡ κλωστή (í klostí)
tight, σφιχτό (sfihtó)
tie, ἡ γραβάτα (í ghraváta)
tobacco, ὁ καπνός (ó kapnós)
tobacco pouch, ἡ καπνοσακκούλα (í kapnosakoóla)
torch, ὁ φακός (ó fakós)
toy, τό παιχνίδι (tó pehníthi)

umbrella, ἡ ὀμπρέλλα (í ombrélla)
wallet, τό πορτοφόλι (tó portofóli)
watch, τό ρολόϊ (tó rolóy)
wide, φαρδύ (farthí)
wire, τό σύρμα (tó sírma)
wood, τό ξύλο (tó ksílo)
wool, τό μαλλί (tó malí)
writing-paper, τό μπλόκ (tó blók)

I want to buy . . .	Θέλω ν'ἀγοράσω . . .
	thélo naghoráso . . .
Do you sell . . .?	Πουλᾶτε . . .;
	pooláte . . .?
Where is the market?	Ποῦ εἶναι ἡ ἀγορά;
	poó íne i aghorá?
Have you anything cheaper (better)?	Ἔχετε τίποτα φθηνότερο (καλύτερο);
	éhete típota fthinótero (kalítero)?
I want something like this (that).	Θέλω κάτι σάν κι'αὐτό (ἐκεῖνο).
	thélo káti sán kyaftó (ekíno)
Have you anything bigger (smaller, thicker, thinner)?	Ἔχετε τίποτα μεγαλύτερο (μικρότερο, πιό χονδρό, λεπτότερο);
	éhete típota meghalítero (mikrótero, pyó hondró, leptótero)?
I prefer something in silk (wool, cotton, nylon).	Προτιμῶ κάτι σέ μεταξωτό (μάλλινο, βαμβακερό, νάϋλον).
	protimó káti sé metaksotó (málino, vamvakeró, ná-ilon)
How much does it cost a metre?	Πόσο κάνει τό μέτρο;
	póso káni tó métro?
	(*Cloth is sold by the metre*=39″)
What width is it?	Τί φάρδος ἔχει;
	tí fárthos éhi?
What size?	Τί νούμερο; (μέγεθος)
	tí noómero (méyethos)?
Have you nothing longer (shorter)?	Ἔχετε τίποτα μακρύτερο (κοντώτερο);
	éhete típota makrítero (kondótero)?

Can you order it for me? Μοῦ τό παραγγέλνετε;
moó tó parangélnete?

Will you send it to this address? Μπορεῖτε νά τό στείλετε σ'αὐτή τή διεύθυνση;
boríte ná tó stílete saftí tí thiéfthinsi?

Can you make me a parcel? Μοῦ τό κάνετε ἕνα δέμα;
moó tó kánete éna théma?

I shall take them now. Θά τά πάρω τώρα.
thá tá páro tóra

Have you a carrier bag? Ἔχετε χαρτοσακκοῦλες;
éhete hartosakoóles?

Have you a piece of string? Ἔχετε σπάγγο;
éhete spángo?

That's exactly what I want. Εἶναι αὐτό ἀκριβῶς πού θέλω.
íne aftó akrivós poó thélo.

Pay at the cash desk, please. Πληρώνετε στό ταμεῖο, παρακαλῶ.
plirónete stó tamío, parakaló
(*In many shops one pays at the cash desk and collects one's purchase at a delivery counter, called* παραλαβή (paralaví)

You have given me the wrong change. Τά ρέστα δέν εἶναι σωστά.
tá résta thén íne sostá

May I leave this here for a while? Μπορῶ νά τ'ἀφήσω ἐδῶ γιά λίγο;
boró ná tafíso ethó yá lígho?

I will collect it in an hour. Θά τό πάρω σέ μιά ὥρα.
thá tó páro sé miá óra

Can you match this colour? Μπορεῖτε νά βρῆτε τέτοιο χρῶμα;
boríte ná vríte tétyo hróma?

This colour is too loud. Αὐτό τό χρῶμα εἶναι πολύ χτυπητό.
aftó tó hróma íne polí htipitó

Show me something quieter. Δεῖξτε μου κάτι πιό σοβαρό.
thíkstemoo káti pyó sovaró

I bought this two days ago (yesterday).
Τό ἀγόρασα πρίν δυό μέρες (χθές).
to aghórasa prín thió méres (hthés)

It doesn't work.
Δέν δουλεύει.
thén thoolévi

It is broken (torn, stained).
Εἶναι σπασμένο (σχισμένο, λερωμένο).
íne spazméno (skhizméno, leroméno)

It doesn't fit me.
Δέν μοῦ χωράει.
thén moó horái

Can you change it?
Μπορεῖτε νά τό ἀλλάξετε;
boríte ná tó aláksete?

Can you refund my money?
Ἐπιστρέφετε χρήματα;
epistréfete hrímata?

You have not sent ...
Δέν στείλατε τό ...
thén stílate tó ...

I have not received ...
Δέν ἔλαβα ...
thén élava ...

Here is my address.
Αὐτή εἶναι ἡ διεύθυνσή μου.
aftí íne í thiéfthinsímoo

Will you give me a reduction?
Θά μοῦ κάνετε ἔκπτωση;
thá moó kánete ékptosi?

It is very expensive. I will give you sixty drachmas.
Εἶναι ἀκριβό. Θά σᾶς δώσω ἑξῆντα δρχ.
íne akrivó.   thá sás thíno eksínta thrahmés

Do you sell English cigarettes (tobacco)?
Πουλᾶτε ἀγγλικά τσιγάρα (καπνό);
pooláte angliká tsighára (kapnó)?

Where can I buy ...?
Ποῦ μπορῶ νά βρῶ ...;
poó boró ná vró ...?

Is it far from here?
Εἶναι μακρυά ἀπ'ἐδῶ;
íne makryá apethó?

Will you write the name of the shop, please.
Μοῦ γράφετε τό ὄνομα τοῦ καταστήματος, παρακαλῶ;
moó ghráfete tó ónoma toó katastímatos, parakaló?

Where are the antique | Ποῦ εἶναι τά καταστήματα μέ
shops? | τίς ἀντίκες;
poó íne tá katastímata mé tís andíkes?

REPAIRS

I have broken (torn) ... | Ἔσπασα (ἔσκισα) ...
éspasa (éskisa) ...

Can you repair ...? | Διορθώνετε ...;
thiorthónete ...?

When will it be ready? | Πότε θᾶναι ἕτοιμο;
póte tháne étimo?

How much will it be? | Πόσο θά κοστίσει;
póso thá kostísi?

Can you mend it for to-morrow? | Μπορεῖ νᾶναι ἕτοιμο γιά αὔριο;
borí náne étimo yá ávrio?

Can you let me have it by ...? | Μπορῶ νά τό πάρω τήν ...;
boró ná tó páro tín ...?

I have to leave on ... | Θά φύγω τήν ...
thá fígho tín ...

I want it by the end of the week. | Τό χρειάζομαι γιά τό τέλος τῆς ἑβδομάδας.
tó hriázome yá tó télos tís evthomáthas

My watch needs cleaning. | Τό ρολόϊ μου θέλει καθάρισμα.
tó rolóymoo théli kathárizma

The main-spring is broken. | Ἔσπασε τό ἐλατήριο.
éspase tó elatírio

Can you patch this tear (stitch this)? | Μπορεῖτε νά τό μπαλώσετε; (νά τό ράψετε);
boríte ná tó balósete (ná tó rápsete)?

Can you darn this (invisi-bly)? | Μπορεῖτε νά τό καρικώσετε (χωρίς νά φαίνεται);
boríte ná tó karikósete (horís ná fénete)?

Will you sole (heel) these shoes. Θέλω σόλες (τακούνια) στά παπούτσια.

thélo sóles (takoónya) stá papoótsya

Where can I have this mended? Ποῦ μπορῶ νά τό διορθώσω;

poó boró ná tó thiorthóso?

COLOURS

beige, μπέζ (béz)
black, μαῦρο (mávro)
blue, μπλέ (blé)
brown, καφέ (kafé)
dark, σκοῦρο (skoóro)
green, πράσινο (prásino)
grey, γκρί (grí)
ivory, ἰβουάρ (ivooár)
light, ἀνοιχτό (anihtó)
mauve, μώβ (móv)
orange, πορτοκαλλί (portokalí)
pink, ρόζ (róz)
red, κόκκινο (kókino)
white, ἄσπρο (áspro)
yellow, κίτρινο (kítrino)

CLOTHES

blouse, ἡ μπλούζα (í bloóza)
braces, οἱ τιράντες (í tirándes)
cap, ἡ τραγιάσκα (í trayáska)
clothes, τά ροῦχα (tá roóha)
coat, τό παλτό (tó paltó)
dress, τό φόρεμα (tó fórema)
fur, ἡ γούνα (í ghoóna)
gloves, τά γάντια (tá ghándia)
hat, τό καπέλλο (tó kapélo)
hat (*straw*), ἡ ψάθα (í psátha)
heel, τό τακούνι (tó takoóni)
sandals, τά πέδιλα (ta péthila)
shawl, τό σάλι (tó sáli)
skirt, ἡ φούστα (í foósta)
slippers, οἱ παντόφλες (í pandófles)
sole, ἡ σόλα (í sóla)
tie, ἡ γραβάτα (í ghraváta)
undies, τά ἐσώρουχα (tá esórooha)

What is your size? Τί νούμερο φορᾶτε;

tí noómero foráte?

I don't know.	Δέν ξέρω.
	thén kséro
May I try it?	Νά τό δοκιμάσω;
	ná tó thokimáso?
This is too wide (narrow, short, long, big, small).	Εἶναι πολύ φαρδύ (στενό, κοντό, μακρύ, μεγάλο, μικρό).
	íne polí farthí (stenó, kondó, makrí, meghálo, mikró)
These heels are too high.	Τά τακούνια εἶναι πολύ ψηλά.
	tá takoónya íne polí psilá
I want a beach outfit.	Θέλω ἕνα ἀνσάμπλ μπάνιου.
	thélo éna ansámbl bányoo
I would like to see some hand-embroidered skirts.	Μπορῶ νά δῶ φούστες μέ κέντημα χεριοῦ;
	boró ná thó foóstes mé kéndima heryoó?
Show me some hand-woven stuffs.	Θέλω ὑφαντά χειροποίητα.
	thélo ífanda hiropí-ita

FOOD

N.B. *For main vocabulary see under* RESTAURANT: Food, *page 37. Many articles of food are sold by the kilo (2 lb. 3 oz.), including liquids, of which one kilo equals approximately 1¾ pints.*

biscuits, τά μπισκότα (ta biskóta)
butter (*local, European*), τό βούτυρο (ντόπιο, εὐρωπαϊκό) (to voótiro (dópyo, evropa-ikó))
chocolate (*milk, plain*), σοκολάτα (γάλακτος, σκέτη) (i sokoláta (ghálaktos, skéti))
luncheon meat, τό ζαμπόν (τό zambón)
packet, τό πακέτο (τό pakéto)
peppermints, οἱ μέντες (í méndes)
sardines, οἱ σαρδέλλες (í sarthéles)
sweets, οἱ καραμέλες (í karaméles)
tin, τό κουτί (τό kootí)

I want a kilo (half-kilo) of . . .	Θέλω ἕνα κιλό (μισό-κιλό) . . .
	thélo éna kiló (misó-kiló) . . .
How much is it per kilo?	Πόσο κάνει τό κιλό;
	póso káni tó kiló?

A quarter of a kilo of fresh　Ἕνα τέταρτο φρέσκο βούτυρο,
butter, please.　　　　　　παρακαλῶ.
　　　　　　　éna tétarto frésko voótiro, parakaló

These are not ripe (fresh).　Αὐτά δέν εἶναι γινομένα
　　　　　　　　　　　　　　　(φρέσκα).
　　　　　aftá thén íne yinoména (fréska)

Let me choose my own.　　Θέλω νά διαλέξω μόνη (μόνος)
　　　　　　　　　　　　　　μου.
　　　　thélo ná thialékso móni (mónos)moo

Give me a bottle of wine.　Θέλω ἕνα μπουκάλι κρασί.
　　　thélo éna bookáli krasí

It is ... drachmas a bottle.　Ἔχει ... ἡ μπουκάλα.
　　　　　　éhi ... i bookála

N.B. *The drachma is, of course, the Greek unit of currency, but in colloquial speech—
especially in a street market—certain other terms will be heard, e.g.*

μία thekára, thío thekáres, etc.　μία δεκάρα, δύο δεκάρες κ.τ.λ.
(*a* thekára *is one tenth of a drachma*)
éna frángko, ἕνα φράγκο, *means one drachma.*
éna thífrangko, ἕνα δίφραγκο, *means two drachmas.*
éna táliro, ἕνα τάλληρο, *means a five-drachma piece.*
éna thekáriko, ἕνα δεκάρικο, *means a ten-drachma piece.*
éna ikosári, ἕνα εἰκοσάρι, *means a twenty-drachma piece.*
éna penindári, ἕνα πενηντάρι, *means a fifty-drachma note,* **but,**
éna penindaráki, ἕνα πενηνταράκι, *means half a drachma, fifty lepta.*

ACCIDENT AND ILLNESS

VOCABULARY

PARTS OF THE BODY

abdomen, ἡ κοιλία (í kilya)
ankle, ὁ ἀστράγαλος (ó astrághalos)
arm, τό χέρι, ὁ βραχίονας (tó héri, ó vrahíonas)
back, ἡ πλάτη (í pláti)
backbone, ἡ σπονδυλική στήλη (í sponthilikí stíli)
blood, τό αἷμα (tó éma)
body, τό σῶμα (tó sóma)
bone, τό κόκκαλο (tó kókalo)
bowels, τά ἔντερα (tá éndera)
cheek, τό μάγουλο (tó mághoolo)
chest, τό στῆθος (tó stíthos)

chin, τό σαγόνι (tó saghóni)
ear, τό αὐτί (tó aftí)
elbow, ὁ ἀγκώνας (ó angónas)
eye, τό μάτι (tó máti)
eyelid, τό ματοτσίνορο, τό βλέφαρο (tó matotsínoro, to vléfaro)
face, τό πρόσωπο (tó prósopo)
finger, τό δάκτυλο (tó **th**áktilo)
foot, τό πόδι (tó pó**thi**)
gum, τό οὗλον (tó oólon)
hair (*one*), ἡ τρίχα (í tríha)
hair (*all of it*), τά μαλλιά (tá malyá)
hand, τό χέρι (tó héri)
head, τό κεφάλι (tó kefáli)
heart, ἡ καρδιά (í karthyá)
heel, ἡ φτέρνα (í ftérna)
hip, τό ἰσχίον (tó iskhíon)
jaw, τό σαγώνι (tó saghóni)
joint, ἡ κλείδωσις (í klí**th**osis)
kidney, τό νεφρό (tó nefró)
knee, τό γόνατο (tó ghónato)
knee-cap, ἡ ἐπιγονατίς (í epighonatís)
leg, τό πόδι (tó pó**thi**)
lip, τό χεῖλος (tó hílos)
liver, τό σηκότι (tó sikóti)
lung, ὁ πνεύμονας (ó pnévmonas)
mouth, τό στόμα (tó stóma)
muscle, ὁ μῦς (ó mís)
neck, ὁ λαιμός (ó lemós)
nerve, τό νεῦρο (tó névro)
nose, ἡ μύτη (í míti)
rib, τό πλευρό (tó plevró)
shoulder, ὁ ὦμος (ó ómos)
skin, τό δέρμα (tó **th**érma)
skull, τό κρανίο (tó kranío)
stomach, τό στομάχι (tó stomáhi)
throat, ὁ λαιμός (ó lemós)
toe, τό δάκτυλο ποδιοῦ (tó **th**áktilo pothyoó)
tongue, ἡ γλῶσσα (í ghlósa)
tonsil, ἡ ἀμυγδαλή (í amigh**th**alí)
tooth, τό δόντι (tó **th**óndi)
false teeth (**plate**), ἡ μασέλλα (i maséla)
vein, ἡ φλέβα (í fléva)
wrist, ὁ καρπός (ó karpós)

GENERAL

abscess, τό ἀπόστημα (tó apóstima)
accident, τό δυστύχημα (tó thistíhima)
ache, ὁ πόνος (ó pónos)
ambulance, τό ἀσθενοφόρο (tó asthenofóro)

appendicitis, ὁ σκωληκοειδῖτις (ό skoliko-ithítis)
bandage, ὁ ἐπίδεσμος (ὁ epíthezmos)
bite (*dog*), τό δάγκωμα (to thángkoma), (*insect*) τό τσίμπημα (tó tsímbima)
blister, ἡ φουσκάλα (í fooskála)
boil, τό σπειρί (tó spirí)
bruise, ἡ ἐκχύμωση (í ekhímosi)
burn, τό κάψιμο (tó kápsimo)
chill, τό κρυολόγημα (tó kriolóyima)
chiropodist, ὁ θεραπευτής τῶν κάλων (o therapeftís tón kálon)
cold, τό κρύωμα (tó kríoma)
constipation, ἡ δυσκοιλιότητα (í thiskiliótita)
consultation, ἡ συμβουλή (í simvoolí)
convalescence, ἡ ἀνάρρωση (í anárosi)
convulsion, ὁ σπασμός (ό spazmós)
corn, ὁ κάλος (ό kálos)
cough, ὁ βῆχας (ό víhas)
cramp, ἡ κράμπα (í krámba)
cure, ἡ θεραπεία (í therapía)
cure, to, θεραπεύω (therapéno)
cut, scratch, τό κόψιμο, τό γρατσούνισμα (tó kópsimo, tó ghrats-oónizma)
dentist, ὁ ὀδοντογιατρός (ό othondoyatrós)
diarrhoea, ἡ διάρροια (í thiária)
diet, ἡ δίαιτα (í thíeta)
dizziness, ἡ ζαλάδα (í zalátha)
doctor, ὁ γιατρός (ό yatrós)
epidemic, ἡ ἐπιδημία (í epithimía)
faint, ἡ λιποθυμία (í lipothimía)
faint, to, λιποθυμῶ (lipothimó)
fever, ὁ πυρετός (ό piretós)
filling, stopping, τό σφράγισμα (tó sfráyizma)
First Aid Service, αἱ Πρῶται Βοήθειαι (é próte vo-íthie)
fracture, τό σπάσιμο (tó spásimo)
hay-fever, ἡ ἀλεργία (í aleryía)
headache, ὁ πονοκέφαλος (ό ponokéfalos)
health, ἡ ὑγεία (í iyía)
hiccups, ὁ λόξυγκας (ό lóksingas)
hospital, τό νοσοκομεῖο (tó nosokomío)
illness, ἡ ἀσθένεια, ἡ ἀρρώστια (í asthénia, i aróstia)
indigestion, ἡ δυσπεψία (í thispepsía)
influenza, ἡ γρίππη (í ghrípi)
injection, ἡ ἔνεση (í énesi)
insomnia, ἡ ἀϋπνία (í aipnía)
itch, ἡ φαγούρα (í faghoóra)
nausea, ἡ ναυτία (í naftía)
nurse, ἡ νοσοκόμα (í nosokóma)
operation, ἡ ἐγχείρηση (í enghírisi)
pain, ὁ πόνος (ό pónos)

patient, ὁ ἀσθενής (ó asthenís)
poison, τό δηλητήριο (tó thilitírio)
policeman, ὁ ἀστυνομικός (ó astinomikós)
remedy, τό φάρμακο (tó fármako)
scar, τό σημάδι (tó simáthi)
sick, to feel, ἀνακατεύομαι (anakatévome)
sea-sickness, ἡ ναυτία (í naftía)
sling, ἡ χειρουργική ταινία (í hirooryikí tenía)
splint, ὁ νάρθηκας (ó nárthikas)
spot, τό σπειρί (tó spirí)
sprain, τό στραμπούλιγμα (tó straboólighma)
sting, τό τσίμπημα (tó tsímbima)
stitch, τό ράψιμο (tó rápsimo)
stomach-ache, ὁ στομαχόπονος (ó stomahóponos)
stye, τό κριθαράκι (tó kritharáki)
sunstroke, ἡ ἡλίαση (í ilíasi)
sunburn, τό ἡλιόκαμα (tó ilíokama)
surgeon, ὁ χειρουργός (ó hiroorghós)
surgery (*doctor's office*), τό ἰατρεῖον (tó yatríon)
swelling, τό πρήξιμο (tó príksimo)
swell, to, πρήζομαι (prízome)
temperature (*fever*), ὁ πυρετός (ó piretós)
throat, ὁ λαιμός (ó lemós)
toothache, ὁ πονόδοντος (ó ponóthondos)
treatment, ἡ θεραπεία (í therapía)
vomit, to, κάνω ἐμετό (káno emetó)
wound, τό τραῦμα (tó trávma)
X-ray, ἡ ἀκτινοσκόπισις (i aktinoskópisis)

There has been an accident. Ἔγινε δυστύχημα.
éyine thistíhima

Call a policeman quickly. Καλέσατε γρήγορα ἕναν ἀστυνομικό.
kalésate ghríghora énan astinomikó

Call an ambulance (the First Aid Service). Καλέσατε τό αὐτοκίνητο τῶν Πρώτων Βοηθειῶν.
kalésate tó aftokínito tón próton voythyón

He must not be moved. It is very dangerous. Δέν πρέπει νά κινηθῆ. Εἶναι πολύ ἐπικίνδυνο.
thén prépi ná kinithí. íne polí epikínthino

Is there a doctor near here? Ὑπάρχει γιατρός ἐδῶ κοντά;
ipárhi yatrós ethó kondá?

Someone has fallen in the water. Κάποιος ἔπεσε στή θάλασσα.
kápyos épese stí thálasa

He needs artificial respira-   Χρειάζεται τεχνητή ἀναπνοή.
tion.
                                 hriázete tehnití anapnoí

He is seriously injured.   Εἶναι βαρειά τραυματισμένος.
                                 íne varyá travmatizménos

He has been knocked down.   Τόν παρέσυρε αὐτοκίνητο.
                                 tón parésire aftokiníto

He is losing blood.   Χάνει αἶμα.
                                 háni éma

He has lost consciousness.   Εἶναι σέ ἀφασία.
                                 íne sé afasía

He has fainted.   Λιποθύμησε.
                                 lipothímise

He has burnt (cut) his face.   Κάηκε (κόπηκε) στό πρόσωπο.
                                 káike (kópike) stó prósopo

It is bleeding.   Ἔχει αἱμορραγία.
                                 éhi emorayía

It is swollen.   Πρήστηκε.
                                 prístike

Who is responsible for the   Ποιός εὐθύνεται γιά τό δυστύ-
accident?   χημα;
                                 pyós efthínete yá tó thistíhima?

Are there any witnesses?   Ὑπάρχουν μάρτυρες;
                                 ipárhoon mártires?

Have you any bandages?   Ἔχετε ἐπιδέσμους;
                                 éhete epithézmoos?

Can you dress this wound?   Μπορεῖτε νά δέσετε αὐτή τήν
                                                            πληγή;
                                 boríte ná thésete aftí tín pliyí?

Can you make a splint?   Μπορεῖτε νά φτιάξετε νάρθηκα;
                                 boríte ná ftiáksete nárthika?

Bring some hot (cold) water   Φέρετε λίγο ζεστό (κρῦο) νερό
(a blanket).   (μιά κουβέρτα).
                                 férete lígho zestó (krío) neró (miá koovérta)

Can we get a stretcher?   Μπορεῖτε νά βρῆτε φορεῖο;
                                 boríte ná vríte forío?

Help me to carry him (her). Βοηθῆστε με νά τόν (τήν)
μεταφέρουμε.
voithíste me ná tón (tín) metaféroome

He is not feeling well. Δέν αἰσθάνεται καλά.
thén esthánete kalá

I do not feel at all well. Δέν αἰσθάνομαι καθόλου καλά.
Please send for the doctor. Παρακαλῶ, φωνάζετε τό γιατρό;
thén esthánome kathóloo kalá. parakaló, fonázete tó yatró?

I am suffering from my . . . Ὑποφέρω ἀπό . . .
ipoféro apó . . .

I have a pain in . . . Ἔχω πόνο στό . . .
ého póno stó . . .

Do you feel any pain here? Πονᾶτε ἐδῶ;
ponáte ethó?

I have pains all over. Πονάω παντοῦ.
ponáo pandoó

Show me your tongue. Δεῖξτε μου τή γλῶσσα σας.
thíkstemoo tí ghlósasas

When did it happen (start)? Πότε ἔγινε (ἄρχισε);
póte éyine (árhise)?

How often do you feel it? Κάθε πότε τόν νοιώθετε;
káthe póte tó nyóthete?

He is not sleeping well. Δέν κοιμᾶται καλά.
thén kimáte kalá

He cannot eat. Δέν μπορεῖ νά φάη.
thén borí ná fái

I have no appetite. I have Δέν ἔχω ὄρεξη. Ἔχω δυσπεψία.
indigestion.
then ého óreksi. ého thispepsía

My stomach is upset. Ἔχω τό στομάχι μου.
ého tó stomáhimoo

He has (I have) a tempera- Ἔχει (ἔχω) πυρετό.
ture.
éhi (ého) piretó

I am going to see the doctor. Θά πάω στό γιατρό.
thá páo stó yatró

I have caught a cold.	Ἔχω κρυολόγημα.
	ého kriolóyima
My nose is bleeding.	Ἄνοιξε ἡ μύτη μου.
	ánikse i mítimoo
I have a bad cough.	Ἔχω ἄσχημο βήχα.
	ého áskhimo víha
I feel giddy.	Ζαλίζομαι.
	zalízome
I keep vomiting.	Κάνω συνέχεια ἐμετό.
	káno sinéhia emetó
I think I have food poisoning.	Νομίζω πώς ἔχω τροφική δηλητηρίαση.
	nomízo pós ého trofikí thilitiríasi
What have you eaten?	Τί φάγατε;
	tí fághate
I have diarrhoea.	Ἔχω διάρροια.
	ého thiária
I have been stung by a bee (wasp).	Μέ τσίμπησε μέλισσα (σφῆκα).
	mé tsíbise mélisa (sfíka)
I have trodden on a sea-urchin.	Πάτησα ἀχινό.
	pátisa ahinó
I have been bitten by a dog.	Μέ δάγκωσε σκῦλος.
	mé thángose skílos
What must I do?	Τί πρέπει νά κάνω;
	tí prépi ná káno?
Should I stay in bed?	Πρέπει νά μείνω στό κρεβάτι;
	prépi ná míno stó kreváti?
Will you give me a prescription?	Θά μοῦ δώσετε συνταγή;
	thá moó thósete sintayí?
I feel much better.	Νοιώθω καλύτερα.
	nyótho kalítera
When will you come and see me again?	Πότε θά ξανάρθετε νά μέ δεῖτε;
	póte thá ksanárthete ná mé thíte?

What is your charge, doctor? Τί σᾶς χρωστάω γιατρέ;

tí sás hrostáo yatré?

Where can I have this prescription made up? Ποῦ μπορῶ νά φτιάξω αὐτή τή συνταγή;

poó boró ná ftiákso aftí tí sindayí?

Can you recommend a dentist? Ἔχετε κανένα ὀδοντογιατρό νά μοῦ συστήσετε;

éhete kanéna othondoyatró ná moó sistísete?

I want to make an appointment for ... Θέλω νά κλείσω ραντεβοῦ γιά ...

thélo ná klíso randevoó yá ...

I have toothache. Ἔχω πονόδοντο.

ého ponóthondo

Which tooth aches? Ποιό δόντι πονάει;

pyó thóndi ponái?

This one. Αὐτό ἐδῶ.

aftó ethó

Are you going to fill it (take it out)? Θά τό σφραγίσετε (θά τό βγάλετε);

thá tó sfrayísete? (thá tó vghálete?)

I have lost a stopping. Μοῦφυγε τό σφράγισμα.

moófiye tó sfráyizma

I want to have this tooth taken out. Θέλω νά βγάλω αὐτό τό δόντι.

thélo ná vghálo aftó tó thóndi

Can you save it? Θά τό σώσουμε;

thá tó sósoome?

You are hurting me. Μέ πονᾶτε.

mé ponáte

Open wide. Rinse. A little wider. Ἀνοῖξτε. Ξεβγᾶλτε. Ποιό ἀνοιχτά.

aníkste. ksevghálte. pyó anihtá.

Don't close your mouth till I tell you. Μήν κλείσετε τό στόμα σας ὥσπου νά σᾶς πῶ.

mí klísete tó stómasas óspoo ná sás pó

Does that hurt? Πονάει αὐτό;
ponái aftó?

Grind your teeth very gently. Τρῖψτε τά δόντια σας ἐλαφρά.
trípste tá thóndiasas elafrá

Will you give me an injection? Θά μοῦ κάνετε ἔνεση;
thá moó kánete énesi?

My gums are very swollen (are bleeding). Τά οὖλα μου εἶναι πρήσμένα (ματώνουν).
tá oólamoo íne prizména (matónoon)

This tooth is hollow and the nerve exposed. Τό δόντι αὐτό εἶναι τρύπιο, φαίνεται τό νεῦρο.
tó thóndi aftó íne trípio, fénete tó névro

My plate hurts. Πονάει ἡ μασέλλα μου.
ponái í masélamoo

I have broken my plate. Can you repair it? Ἔσπασα τή μασέλλα μου. Μπορεῖτε νά τή διορθώσετε;
éspasa tí masélamoo. boríte ná tí thiorthósete?

Don't bite on that for four hours. Μή μασάτε ἀπ'ἐδῶ γιά τέσσερις ὥρες.
mí masáte apethó yá téseris óres

COUNTRIES AND NATIONALITIES

Country

Africa, ἡ ᾿Αφρική (í afrikí)
Albania, ἡ ᾿Αλβανία (í alvanía)
America, ἡ ᾿Αμερική (í amerikí)
Asia, ἡ ᾿Ασία (í asía)
Australia, ἡ Αὐστραλία (í afstralía)
Belgium, τό Βέλγιο (tó vélyo)
Brazil, ἡ Βραζιλία (í vrazilía)
Bulgaria, ἡ Βουλγαρία (í voolgharía)
Canada, ὁ Καναδᾶς (ó kanathás)
China, ἡ Κίνα (í kína)
Cyprus, ἡ Κύπρος (í kípros)
Czechoslovakia, ἡ Τσεχοσλοβακία (i tschoslovakía)
Denmark, ἡ Δανία (i thanía)
Egypt, ἡ Αἴγυπτος (í éyiptos)
England, ἡ ᾿Αγγλία (í anglía)
Finland, ἡ Φιλανδία (í filanthía)

France, ἡ Γαλλία (í ghalía)
Germany, ἡ Γερμανία (í yermanía)
Greece, ἡ Ἑλλάδα (í elátha)
Holland, ἡ Ὁλλανδία (í olanthía)
India, ἡ Ἰνδία (i inthía)
Ireland, ἡ Ἰρλανδία (í irlanthía)
Italy, ἡ Ἰταλία (í italía)
Japan, ἡ Ἰαπωνία (í iaponía)
Jugoslavia, ἡ Γιουγκοσλαβία (í yoogoslavía)
New Zealand, ἡ Νέα Ζηλανδία (í néa zilanthía)
Norway, ἡ Νορβηγία (í norviyía)
Portugal, ἡ Πορτογαλλία (í portoghalía)
Russia, ἡ Ρωσσία (í rosía)
Turkey, ἡ Τουρκία (í toorkía)
Scotland, ἡ Σκωτία (í skotía)
Spain, ἡ Ἰσπανία (í ispanía)
Sweden, ἡ Σουηδία (í swithía)
Switzerland, ἡ Ἑλβετία (í elvetía)
U.N.O., τά Ἡνωμένα Ἔθνη, ΟΗΕ
U.S.A., οἱ Ἡνωμένες Πολιτεῖες Ἀμερικῆς,
    ΗΠΑ
U.S.S.R., ἡ Ἔνωση Σοβιετικῶν Σοσιαλισ-
    τικῶν Δημοκρατιῶν, ΕΣΣΔ
Wales, ἡ Οὐαλλία (í walía)

INHABITANTS

		M.	F.	
African	Ἀφρικαν	-ός	-ίδα	(africanós, africanítha)
Albanian	Ἀλβαν	-ός	-ίδα	(alvanós, alvanítha)
American	Ἀμερικαν	-ός	-ίδα	(americanós, americanítha)
Asian	Ἀσιάτ	-ις	-ισσα	(asyátis, asyátissa)
Australian	Αὐστραλ	-ός	-ίδα	(afstralós, afstralítha)
Belgian	Βέλγ	-ος	-ίδα	(vélghos, velyítha)
Brazilian	Βραζιλι	-ανός	-άνα	(vrazilyanós, vrazilyána)
Bulgarian	Βούλγαρ	-ος	-άρα	(voólgharos, voolghára)
Canadian	Καναδ	-ός	-ή	(kanathós, kanathí)
Chinese	Κινέζ	-ος	-α	(kinézos, kinéza)
Cypriot	Κύπρι	-ος	-α	(kíprios, kipría)
Czechoslovak	Τσεχοσλοβάκ	-ος	-α	(tsehoslovákos, tsehoslováka)
Dane	Δαν	-ός	-έζα	(thanós, thanéza)
Egyptian	Αἰγύπτ	-ιος	-ία	(eyíptios, eyiptía)
Englishman	Ἄγγλ	-ος	-ίδα	(ánglos, anglítha)
(also often):	Ἐγγλέζ	-ος	-α	(englézos, engléza)
Finn	Φιλλανδ	-ός	-έζα	(filanthós, filanthéza)
Frenchman	Γάλλ	-ος	-ίδα	(ghálos, ghalítha)
German	Γερμαν	-ός	-ίδα	(yermanós, yermanítha)
Greek	Ἕλλην	-ας	-ίδα	(éllinas, ellinítha)

Dutchman	Ὁλλανδ	-ός	-έζα	(olanthós, olanthéza)
Indian	Ἰνδ	-ός	-ή	(inthós, inthí)
Irishman	Ἰρλανδ	-ός	-έζα	(irlanthós, irlanthéza)
Italian	Ἰταλ	-ός	-ίδα	(italós, italítha)
Japanese	Ἰάπων	-ας	-έζα	(yáponas, yaponéza)
New Zealander	Νεο Ζηλανδ	-ός	-έζα	(zilanthós, zilanthéza)
Norwegian	Νορβηγ	-ός	-ίδα	(norvighós, norviyítha)
Portuguese	Πορτογάλλ	-ος	-ίδα	(portoghálos, portoghalítha)
Russian	Ρώσσ	-ος	-ίδα	(rósos, rosítha)
Scot	Σκωτσέζ	-ος	-α	(skotsézos, skotséza)
Spaniard	Ἰσπαν	-ός	-ίδα	(ispanós, ispanítha)
Swede	Σουηδ	-ός	-έζα	(sooithós, sooithéza)
Swiss	Ἑλβετ	-ός	-ίδα	(elvetós, elvetítha)
Turk	Τοῦρκ	-ος	-άλα	(toórkos, toorkála)
Welshman	Οὐαλλ	-ός	-ίδα	(ooalós, ooalítha)
Yugoslav	Γιουγκοσλάβ	-ος	-α	(yoogoslávos, yoogosláva)

GEOGRAPHICAL TERMS AND PLACE NAMES

Aegean, τό Αἰγαῖον (tó eyéon)
Athens, ἡ Ἀθήνα (í athína)
Athos, Mount, ὁ Ἄθως, τό Ἅγιον Ὄρος (ó áthos, tó áyon óros)
bank, ἡ ὄχθη (í óhthi)
bay, ὁ κόλπος (ó kólpos)
beach, ἡ παραλία (í paralía)
canal, ἡ διώρυγα, τό κανάλι (í thíorigha, tó kanáli)
Candia, τό Ἡράκλειον (tó iráklion)
Canea, τά Χανιά (tá hanyá)
cape, τό ἀκρωτήρι (tó akrotíri)
cave, ἡ σπηλιά (í spilyá)
city, ἡ πόλη (í póli)
cliff, ὁ γκρεμός (ó gremós)
coast, ἡ ἀκτή (í aktí)
Corfu, ἡ Κέρκυρα (í kérkira)
county, ἡ χώρα (í hóra)
countryside, ἡ ἐξοχή (í eksohí)
Crete, ἡ Κρήτη (í kríti)
desert, ἡ ἔρημος (í érimos)
east, ἡ Ἀνατολή (í anatolí)
field, τό χωράφι (tó horáfi)
footpath, τό μονοπάτι (tó monopáti)
forest, τό δάσος (tó thásos)
gulf, ὁ κόλπος (ó kólpos)
harbour, τό λιμάνι (tó limáni)
Herakleion, τό Ἡράκλειον (tó iráklion)
island, τό νησί (tó nisí)
lake, ἡ λίμνη (í límni)

land, ἡ ξηρά (í ksirá)
lighthouse, ὁ φάρος (ó fáros)
marsh, τό ἕλος (tó élos)
mountain, τό βουνό (tó voonó)
Mycenae, οἱ Μυκῆνες (í mikínes)
Mitylene, ἡ Μιτυλήνη (í mitilíni)
north, ὁ Βορρᾶς (ó vorás)
path, τό μονοπάτι (tó monopáti)
Peloponnese, ἡ Πελοπόννησος (í pelopónisos)
Piraeus ὁ Πειραιᾶς (ó pireás)
plain, ἡ πεδιάδα (í pethyátha)
port, τό λιμάνι (tó limáni)
Rhodes, ἡ Ρόδος (í róthos)
river, τό ποτάμι (tó potámi)
road, ὁ δρόμος (ó thrómos)
Salonica, ἡ Θεσσαλονίκη (í thesaloníki)
sea, ἡ θάλασσα (í thálasa)
shore, ἡ παραλία (i paralía)
south, ὁ Νότος (ó nótos)
spring, ἡ πηγή (i piyí)
stream, τό ρυάκι (to ryáki)
town, ἡ πόλη (í póli)
valley, ἡ κοιλάδα (í kilátha)
village, τό χωριό (tó horyó)
waterfall, ὁ καταρράκτης (ó kataráktis)
west, ἡ Δύση (í thísi)
wood, τό δάσος (tó thásos)
world, ὁ κόσμος (ó kózmos)

ANIMALS

bedbug, ὁ κοριός (ó koryós)
bird, τό πουλί (tó poolí)
bull, ὁ ταῦρος (ó távros)
butterfly, ἡ πεταλούδα (í petaloótha)
cat, ἡ γάτα (í gháta)
centipede, ἡ σαρανταποδαροῦσα (í sarandapotharoósa)
chicken, τό κοτόπουλο (to kotópoolo)
cockroach, ἡ κατσαρίδα (í katsarítha)
cow, ἡ ἀγελάδα (í ayelátha)
dog, ὁ σκύλος (ó skílos)
donkey, ὁ γάϊδαρος (ó gháitharos)
duck, ἡ πάπια (í pápya)
feather, wing, τό φτερό (tó fteró)
fish, τό ψάρι (tó psári)
fly, ἡ μύγα (í mígha)
fox, ἡ ἀλεποῦ (í alepoó)
goat, ἡ κατσίκα (í katsíka)
goose, ἡ χήνα (í hína)
hen, ἡ κόττα (í kóta)

horse, τό ἄλογο (tó álogho)
insect, τό ἔντομο (tó éndomo)
lamb, τό ἀρνί (tó arní)
lizard, ἡ σαῦρα (í sávra)
mosquito, τό κουνοῦπι (tó koonoópi)
mouse, ὁ ποντικός (ó pondikós)
mule, τό μουλάρι (tó moolári)
owl, ἡ κουκουβάγια (í kookoováya)
ox, τό βῶδι (tó vóthi)
pig, τό γουροῦνι (tó ghooroóni)
rat, ὁ ἀρουραῖος (ó arooréos)
scorpion, ὁ σκορπιός (ó skorpyós)
sheep, τό πρόβατο (tó próvato)
snake, τό φίδι (tó fíthi)
tail, ἡ οὐρά (í oorá)
tortoise, ἡ χελώνα (í helóna)
wolf, ὁ λύκος (ó líkos)

VEGETATION

branch, τό κλαδί (tó klathí)
bush, ὁ θάμνος (ó thámnos)
chestnut, ἡ καστανιά (í kastanyá)
eucalyptus, ὁ εὐκάλυπτος (ó efkáliptos)
flower, τό λουλοῦδι (tó looloóthi)
fruit, τό φροῦτο (tó froóto)
grass, ἡ χλόη (í hló-i)
leaf, τό φῦλλο (tó fílo)
maize, τό καλαμπόκι (tó kalambóki)
oak, ἡ δρῦς (í thrís)
olive, ἡ ἐλῃά (í elyá)
pine, τό πεῦκο (tó péfko)
plane, ὁ πλάτανος (ó plátanos)
plant, τό φυτό (tó fitó)
poplar, ἡ λεύκα (í léfka)
root, ἡ ρίζα (í ríza)
rose, τό τριαντάφυλλο (tó triandáfilo)
tree, τό δέντρο (tó théndro)
trunk, ὁ κορμός (ó kormós)
wheat, τό στάρι (tó stári)
wood, τό δάσος (tó thásos)
vine, τό ἀμπέλι (tó ambéli)

FAMILY AND RELATIONSHIPS

The everyday word is given first, and the one met with on official documents second.

father, ὁ μπαμπάς, ὁ πατέρας (o babás, o patéras)
mother, ἡ μαμά, ἡ μητέρα (i mamá, i mitéra)

husband, ὁ ἄνδρας, ὁ σύζυγος (ó ándras, ó sízighos)
wife, ἡ γυναίκα, ἡ σύζυγος (í yinéka, í sízighos)
son, ὁ γιός (ó yós)
daughter, ἡ κόρη (í kóri)
grandfather, ὁ παππούς (ó papoós)
grandmother, ἡ γιαγιά (í yayá)
grandson, ὁ ἐγγονός (ó enghonós)
granddaughter, ἡ ἐγγονή (í engoní)
uncle, ὁ θεῖος (ó thíos)
aunt, ἡ θεία (í thía)
mother-in-law, ἡ πεθερά (í petherá)
father-in-law, ὁ πεθερός (ó petherós)
son-in-law, ὁ γαμπρός (ó ghabrós)
daughter-in-law, ἡ νύφη (í nífi)
godfather, ὁ νονός (ó nonós)
godmother, ἡ νονά (í noná)
best man, ὁ κουμπάρος (ó koombáros)

(*In Greece, a more important person than in England. He pays for the wedding and acquires a permanent relationship with the family. The feminine equivalent is* ἡ κουμπάρα (*í koombára*).

parents, οἱ γονεῖς (í ghonís)
children, τά παιδιά, τά τέκνα (tá pethyá, tá tékna)
family, ἡ οἰκογένεια (í ikoyénya)
relatives, οἱ συγγενεῖς (í singenís)
niece, ἡ ἀνηψιά (í anipsyá)
nephew, ὁ ἀνηψιός (ó anipsyós)
cousin (*male*), ὁ ξάδελφος (ó ksáthélfos)
cousin (*female*), ἡ ξαδέλφη (í ksathélfi)
friend (*male*), ὁ φίλος (ó fílos)
friend (*female*), ἡ φίλη (í fíli)
acquaintance, ὁ γνωστός, ἡ γνωστὴ (ó ghnostós, í ghností)
brother, ὁ ἀδελφός (ó athelfós)
sister, ἡ ἀδελφή (í athelfí)

MONEY

In Greece the basic unit of currency is the drachma, which is divided into 100 lepta. Banknotes are of 1,000 drachmas, 500 drachmas, 100 drachmas and 50 drachmas. Coins are of 20, 10, 5, 2, 1 and half a drachma, and of 20, 10 and 5 lepta. For colloquial terms for some of these coins, see the section SHOPPING; FOOD.

VOCABULARY

bank, ἡ τράπεζα (í trápeza)
cash, to, ἐξαργυρώνω (eksaryiróno)
change (*returned*), τά ρέστα (tá résta)
change (*small*), τά ψιλά (tá psilá)

cheque, ἡ ἐπιταγή, τό τσέκ (í epitayí, tó tsék)
cheque (*traveller's*), τό ταξιδιωτικό τσέκ (tó taksithiotikó tsék)
coin, τό νόμισμα (tó nómizma)
exchange, τό συνάλλαγμα (tó sinálaghma)
letter of credit, τό πιστωτικόν ἔγγραφο (tó pistotikón éngrafo)
money, τά χρήματα (tá hrímata)
money exchange bureau, τό σαράφικο (tó saráfiko)
note, τό χαρτονόμισμα (tó hartonómizma)
rate, ἡ τιμή συναλλάγματος (í timí sinalághmatos)

Is there a bank near here?   Ὑπάρχει τράπεζα ἐδῶ κοντά;
ipárhi trápeza ethó kondá?

Where can one cash a travel-   Ποῦ μπορῶ ν'ἀλλάξω ἕνα ταξι-
ler's cheque?   διωτικό τσέκ;
poó boró nalákso éna taksithiotikó tsék?

Will you cash this cheque,   Μπορεῖτε νά ἐξαργυρώσετε
please.   αὐτή τήν ἐπιταγή, παρα-
         καλῶ.
boríte ná eksaryirósete aftí tín epitayí, parakaló?

How much is that worth?   Τί ἀξία ἔχει αὐτό;
tí aksía éhi aftó?

What is the rate of exchange   Ποιά εἶναι ἡ τιμή συναλλάγματος
today?   σήμερα;
pya íne í timí sinalághmatos símera?

I have a letter of credit.   Ἔχω πιστωτικόν ἔγγραφο.
     ého pistotikón éngrafo

Can you give me some small   Μπορεῖτε νά κάνετε ψιλά αὐτό
change for 100 drachmas?   τό κατοστάρικο;
boríte ná kánete psilá aftó to katostáriko?

I think there is a mistake in   Νομίζω, ὑπάρχει ἕνα λάθος στό
your calculations.   λογαριασμό.
nomízo, ipárhi éna láthos stó loghariazmó

TABLES

1 drachma =	6d. =	
5 drachmas =	1/- =	
10 drachmas =	2/6 =	
20 drachmas =	5/- =	
50 drachmas =	10/- =	
100 drachmas =	£1 =	
500 drachmas =	£5 =	
1000 drachmas =	£10 =	

(*The traveller may insert the prevailing rates of exchange*)

NUMBERS

(*There are masculine, feminine and neuter forms of many numbers. Before the word* δραχμές (**thrahmés**) *use the feminine, with* -ες)

1 = ἕνας, μία, ἕνα (énas, mía, éna)
2 = δύο (**thío**)
3 = τρεῖς, τρεῖς, τρία (trís, trís, tría)
4 = τέσσερις, τέσσερις, τέσσερα (téseris, téseris, tésera)
5 = πέντε (pénde)
6 = ἕξη (éksi)
7 = ἑπτά (eptá)
8 = ὀκτώ (októ)
9 = ἐννέα (enéa)
10 = δέκα (**théka**)
11 = ἕνδεκα (én**theka**)
12 = δώδεκα (**thótheka**)
13 = δεκατρεῖς (**theka**trís)
14 = δεκατέσσερις (**theka**téseris)
15 = δεκαπέντε (**theka**pénde)
16 = δεκαέξη (**theka**áksi)
17 = δεκαεφτά (**theka**eftá)
18 = δεκαοκτώ (**theka**októ)
19 = δεκαεννέα (**theka**enéa)
20 = εἴκοσι (íkosi)
21 = εἴκοσιένα, εἴκοσιμία (ikosiéna, ikosimía)
22 = εἴκοσιδύο (ikosithío)
23 = εἴκοσιτρεῖς, εἴκοσιτρία (ikositrís, ikositría)
24 = εἴκοσιτέσσερις, εἴκοσιτέσσερα (ikositéseris, ikositésera)
25 = εἴκοσιπέντε (ikosipénde)

26 = εἰκοσιέξη (ikosiéksi)
27 = εἰκοσιεπτά (ikosieptá)
28 = εἰκοσιοκτώ (ikosioktó)
29 = εἰκοσιεννέα (ikosienéa)
30 = τριάντα (triánda)
40 = σαράντα (saránda)
50 = πενήντα (peninda)
60 = ἑξῆντα (eksínda)
70 = ἑβδομήντα (evthomínda)
80 = ὀγδόντα (oghthónda)
90 = ἐνενήντα (enenínda)
100 = ἑκατό (ekató)
200 = διακόσοι, διακόσες, διακόσα (thiakósi, thiakóses, thiakósa)
300 = τρακόσοι (trakósi, etc.)
400 = τετρακόσοι (tetrakósi, etc.)
500 = πεντακόσοι (pendakósi, etc.)
600 = ἑξακόσοι (eksakósi, etc.)
700 = ἑπτακόσοι (eptakósi, etc.)
800 = ὀκτακόσοι (oktakósi, etc.)
900 = ἐννιακόσοι (enyakósi, etc.)
1,000 = χίλιοι, χίλιες, χίλια (híli-i, hílies, hília)
2,000 = δύο χιλιάδες (thío hiliáthes)
3,000 = τρεῖς χιλιάδες (trís hiliáthes)
4,000 = τέσσερις χιλιάδες (téseris hiliáthes)
1,000,000 = ἕνα ἑκατομμύριο (éna ekatomírio)

1st = πρῶτος, πρώτη, πρῶτο (prótos, próti, próto)
2nd = δεύτερος, -η, -ο (théfteros, -i, -o)
3rd = τρίτος, -η, -ο (trítos, -i, -o)
4th = τέταρτος, -η, -ο (tétartos, -i, -o)
5th = πέμπτος, -η, -ο (pémptos, -i, -o)
6th = ἕκτος, -η, -ο (éktos, -i, -o)
7th = ἕβδομος, -η, -ο (évthomos, -i, -o)
8th = ὄγδοος, -η, -ο (óghtho-os, -i, -o)
9th = ἕννατος, -η, -ο (énatos, -i, -o)
10th = δέκατος, -η, -ο (thékatos, -i, -o)

a half = τό μισό (tó misó)
a quarter = τό ἕν τέταρτο (tó éntétarto)
three-quarters = τρία τέταρτα (tría tétarta)
a third = τό ἕν τρίτο (tó éntríto)
two-thirds = δύο τρίτα (thío tríta)

1920 = χίλια ἐννεακόσια εἴκοσι (hília enyakósya íkosi)
1963 = χίλια ἐννεακόσια ἑξῆντα τρία (hília enyakósya eksínda tría)

CONVERSION TABLES

DISTANCE

Kilometres		Miles	Miles		Kilometres
1	approx.	$\frac{5}{8}$	1	approx.	1·6
2	,,	$1\frac{1}{4}$	2	,,	3·2
3	,,	$1\frac{7}{8}$	3	,,	4·8
4	,,	$2\frac{1}{2}$	4	,,	6·4
5	,,	$3\frac{1}{8}$	5	,,	8
6	,,	$3\frac{3}{4}$	6	,,	9·6
7	,,	$4\frac{3}{8}$	7	,,	11·13
8	,,	5	8	,,	12·9
9	,,	$5\frac{5}{8}$	9	,,	14·5
10	,,	$6\frac{1}{4}$	10	,,	16·1
15	,,	$9\frac{3}{8}$	15	,,	24·1
20	,,	$12\frac{1}{2}$	20	,,	32·2
25	,,	$15\frac{5}{8}$	25	,,	40·2
30	,,	$18\frac{3}{4}$	30	,,	48·3
35	,,	$21\frac{7}{8}$	35	,,	56·3
40	,,	25	40	,,	64·4
45	,,	$28\frac{1}{2}$	45	,,	72·4
50	,,	$31\frac{3}{8}$	50	,,	80·5
55	,,	$34\frac{3}{8}$	55	,,	88·5
60	,,	$37\frac{1}{2}$	60	,,	96·6
65	,,	$40\frac{5}{8}$	65	,,	104·6
70	,,	$43\frac{3}{4}$	70	,,	112·7
75	,,	$46\frac{7}{8}$	75	,,	120·7
80	,,	50	80	,,	128·7
85	,,	$53\frac{1}{8}$	85	,,	136·8
90	,,	$56\frac{1}{4}$	90	,,	144·8
95	,,	$59\frac{3}{8}$	95	,,	152·9
100	,,	$62\frac{1}{2}$	100	,,	161

LENGTH

Centimetres		Feet	Inches	Feet	Inches	Centimetres
1	approx.		$\frac{2}{5}$	1	approx.	2·5
5	,,		2	3	,,	7·5
10	,,		4	6	,,	15
15	,,		6	9	,,	22·5
20	,,		8	1	,,	30·5
25	,,		10	1	6 ,,	45·5
50	,,	1	8	2	,,	61
75	,,	2	6	2	6 ,,	75
100 (1 metre)		3	3	3	,,	91·5

ALTITUDE

Metres		Feet	Feet		Metres
25	approx.	82	50	approx.	15
50	,,	164	75	,,	23
75	,,	246	100	,,	31
100	,,	328	250	,,	76
250	,,	820	500	,,	152
500	,,	1,640	1,000	,,	305
1,000	,,	3,281	2,000	,,	610
2,000	,,	6,562	3,000	,,	915
3,000	,,	9,845	4,000	,,	1,220

N.B. *To convert metres roughly to yards multiply by 12 and divide by 11. E.g. 100 metres × 12 = 1,200 ÷ 11 = 109 yards.*

LIQUID MEASURES

Petrol is sold by the gallon. The litre is not used as a term, but liquids such as wine and milk are sold by the kilogram. For water, one kilo = about 1¾ pints, 1 pint = about 0·57 kilos.

WEIGHTS AND MEASURES

depth, τό βάθος (tó váthos)
height, τό ὕψος (tó ípsos)
length, τό μάκρος (tó mákros)
measure, τό μέτρο (tó métro)
measure, to, μετράω (metráo)
thickness, τό πάχος (tó páhos)
weight, τό βάρος (tó város)
width, τό φάρδος (tó fárthos)

How much does ... weigh? Πόσο ζυγίζει ...;

póso ziyízi ...?

What is the depth (height, Τί εἶναι τό βάθος (ὕψος, μάκρος,
length, thickness) of ...? πάχος) τοῦ ...;

tí íne tó váthos (ípsos, mákros, páhos) toó ...?

It is ... metres (centi- Εἶναι ... μέτρα (ἑκατοστά)
metres) by ... metres. ἐπί ... μέτρα.

íne ... métra (ekatostá) epí ... métra

(*It is just possible that the tourist may come across two units now officially superseded: the* oká, *plural* okáthez (ὀκάδες) *a measure of weight equal to* 1·28 kg. *or* 2·82 lb. *and the* píhis (ὁ πῆχυς), *a measure of length, once much used by drapers, equal to about* 25 in. *or* 65 cm.

WEIGHTS

Grammes	Ounces		Ounces	Grammes
50	approx.	1¾	1 approx.	28
100	,,	3½	2 ,,	56
125	,,	4¼	5 ,,	142
250 (éna tétarto)		8¾	8 (½ lb.)	227
500 (misókilo)		1 lb. 1½	12	340
1,000 (éna kiló)		2 lb. 3	16 (1 lb.)	453

Kilos	Pounds		Stones		Kilos
5	approx.	10¾	1	(14 lb.)	6·35
10	,,	21½	7	(98 ,,)	44·5
15	,,	32¼	8	(112 ,,)	51
20	,,	43	9	(126 ,,)	57
25	,,	54¼	10	(140 ,,)	63·5
30	,,	64½	11	(154 ,,)	70
40	,,	86	12	(168 ,,)	76
50	,,	108½	13	(182 ,,)	82·5
75	,,	162¾	14	(196 ,,)	89
100	,,	220	15	(210 ,,)	95

PRESSURE (TYRES)

Lbs. per sq. in.		Kg. per sq. cm.	Kg. per sq. cm.		Lbs. per sq. in.
16	approx.	1·12	1·1	approx.	16·0
18	,,	1·27	1·3	,,	18·5
20	,,	1·41	1·4	,,	19·9
22	,,	1·55	1·6	,,	22·8
24	,,	1·69	1·7	,,	24·2
26	,,	1·83	1·8	,,	25·6
28	,,	1·97	2·0	,,	28·4
30	,,	2·11	2·1	,,	29·9

TEMPERATURE

Fahrenheit °F.	Centigrade °C.
212 (Boiling)	100
104	40
102	38·9
101	38·3
100	37·8
98·4 (Body)	37
97	36·1
86	30
80	26·7
77	25
68	20
64	17·8
59	15
50	10
41	5
32 (Freezing)	0
28	−2
23	−5
18	−8
12	−11
5	−15
0	−18

CLOTHING SIZES

DRESSES AND SUITS (Women)

British	36	38	40	42	44	46
American	34	36	38	40	42	44
Continental	42	44	46	48	50	52

DRESSES AND SUITS (Junior Miss)

British	32	33	35	36	38	39
American	10	12	14	16	18	20
Continental	38	40	42	44	46	48

MEN'S SUITS AND OVERCOATS

British and American	36	38	40	42	44	46
Continental	46	48	50	52	54	56

SHIRTS

British and American	14	$14\frac{1}{2}$	15	$15\frac{1}{2}$	16	$16\frac{1}{2}$	17
Continental	36	37	38	39	41	42	43

SOCKS

British and American	$9\frac{1}{2}$	10	$10\frac{1}{2}$	11	$11\frac{1}{2}$
Continental	38-39	39-40	40-41	41-42	42-43

HATS

British and American	$6\frac{1}{2}$	$6\frac{5}{8}$	$6\frac{3}{4}$	$6\frac{7}{8}$	7	$7\frac{1}{8}$	$7\frac{1}{4}$	$7\frac{3}{8}$	$7\frac{1}{2}$
Continental	53	54	55	56	57	58	59	60	61

SHOES

British and American	3	4	5	6	7	8	9	10
Continental	36	37	38	39	41	42	43	44

STOCKINGS

British and American	8	$8\frac{1}{2}$	9	$9\frac{1}{2}$	10	$10\frac{1}{2}$
Continental	0	1	2	3	4	5

GLOVE sizes are the same in every country.

ΠΙΝΑΞ

INDEX

ΝΟΤΙΟΣ ΕΛΛΑΣ
(SOUTHERN GREECE)

Klímax 1 : 3,500,000
Khiliómetron